The Exceptional Wife

Living by God's Words

BARBARA SPELL

WESTBOW
PRESS®
A DIVISION OF THOMAS NELSON
& ZONDERVAN

This book is a work of non-fiction. Unless otherwise noted, the author
and the publisher make no explicit guarantees as to the accuracy of
the information contained in this book and in some cases, names
of people and places have been altered to protect their privacy.

WestBow Press books may be ordered through booksellers or by contacting:

WestBow Press
A Division of Thomas Nelson & Zondervan
1663 Liberty Drive
Bloomington, IN 47403
www.westbowpress.com
844-714-3454

Because of the dynamic nature of the Internet, any web addresses or
links contained in this book may have changed since publication and
may no longer be valid. The views expressed in this work are solely those
of the author and do not necessarily reflect the views of the publisher,
and the publisher hereby disclaims any responsibility for them.

Any people depicted in stock imagery provided by Getty Images are
models, and such images are being used for illustrative purposes only.
Certain stock imagery © Getty Images.

ISBN: 978-1-6642-1004-2 (sc)
ISBN: 978-1-6642-1005-9 (hc)
ISBN: 978-1-6642-1003-5 (e)

Library of Congress Control Number: 2020920964

Print information available on the last page.

WestBow Press rev. date: 11/16/2020

To my husband, Jack, whom I loved and cherished throughout fifty-eight years of marriage.

Shortly before the final touches were made to this book, Jack went to his home in heaven. Jack had a sincere interest in this book, knowing that the truths in it changed lives and marriages. I consulted him often as I wrote it, and he knew the contents well. He told me more than once that he wanted the book to be published. Thanks to God, Jack's request is now being honored.

Contents

Acknowledgments

I thank God for these gracious men who brought their time, knowledge, and wisdom to this book.

Dick Leggett, president of Derek Prince Ministries. Many years ago Dick volunteered to read my original cumbersome manuscript. Not until then did I realize how much I needed to learn about writing. With skill and patience, Dick taught me.

The Rev. Dr. Buck Oliphant, a retired pastor who years ago asked me to begin a mentoring program at the church. The mentoring led to teaching, and the teaching led to this book. Happily, Buck read through my first long manuscript and gave tremendous input.

The Rev. Leo Schuster, a faithful friend and my former pastor. Lovingly and joyfully, Leo read through the massive original manuscript. Each comment and suggestion was pertinent, and valuable.

The Rev. Dr. Albert Lawrence, my retired former pastor and friend of many years. Since Al is an author himself, it was an added privilege for me that he read both the original manuscript and my final copy. He generously shared his suggestions and expertise.

The Rev. Reagan Cocke, my gracious pastor who took the time to willingly, carefully, and cheerfully read through the finished manuscript. His helpful input was something I gladly heeded.

I also thank Sallie, Jane, Katie, and Carol, who were always an inspiration and welcome source of encouragement when I taught the marriage class. And my heartfelt thanks goes to special friends Dawn, Robin, and Betsy, who were faithful in prayer from the very beginning.

Getting Started

Bid the older women ... to teach what is good, and so train
the young women to love their husbands and children ...
—Titus 2:3–5 (RSV)

As you read the following pages, you might be like my friend who came to a Bible study I taught years ago. To quote her, "I went to that class each week kicking and screaming because I didn't like what I was hearing. Yet because I knew I was hearing truth, I kept going." As she began to embrace the words God spoke, she and her marriage were revitalized.

You, too, might find some of the following chapters worthy of kicking and screaming your way through, but I encourage you to stick with this to the end. God's ways are not easy, but they are perfect. It is never a mistake to do what He says.

This book evolved from that class. It began as a small mentoring program to teach and encourage young women to love their husbands according to Titus 2:3–5. Eventually the class included women of all ages who wanted to know what God says to women about marriage. Some women in the class had good marriages; others had less than good marriages. Many were looking for direction. Most wanted to avoid the mistakes they had seen in other marriages. Several women were single and wanted to get a head start. No doubt some were curious or perhaps skeptical. But we all had one thing in common: we wanted our marriages to be as good as possible. By the grace of God, changed lives and marriages resulted as we learned to follow God's extraordinary ways.

Similarly this book speaks to all women who want to know what

God says to women about marriage. Nevertheless, I have addressed it primarily to wives. What I have written is only a small portion of God's rich truth concerning marriage, but it is what He has shown me. Embracing His words to wives has drawn me closer to Him and my husband. That is my prayer for you.

Although the Titus 2 scripture calls for older women to teach young women to love their husbands and their children, this book is limited to the subject of loving our husbands. When parents love God and each other, they give their children a gift beyond measure— the enduring picture of love.

In no way is this message meant to place the responsibility for a good marriage on only the wife's shoulders. Instead, it is intended to encourage wives to hear and embrace what God says to *them*. That is our peace, even when or if our husbands are not hearing or accepting what God says to *them*. The Lord is shaping us into exceptional wives.

To all the dear women from the class, thank you for your support and encouragement. How I loved being with you each Monday morning!

Excluded from this book's teaching are situations in which a wife finds herself or her children in a dangerous or life-threatening position. In that case, counsel and protection should be sought along with fervent prayer. Abuse is not to be tolerated.

Marriage Takes Three

Unless the Lord builds the house, They labor in vain who build it.
—Psalm 127:1a

Married!

"I do promise to love and to cherish … as long as I live." Wedding vows. Sincere words saturated with joy, anticipation, and hope. Profound words we will keep. We are in love. Keeping our promise to forever love and cherish our husbands will come easily. And naturally. Really?

Not really. What comes easily and naturally is focusing on ourselves instead of each other. What we want, think, or feel is paramount. The same is true for our husbands. I remember the day a friend said to me, "I was furious at my husband and his ridiculous point of view. I stormed back to the bedroom full of anger. And then it hit me. My husband was as convinced he was right as I was convinced I was right. Furthermore I realized he was just as entitled to have me hear and respect his opinion as I was entitled to have him hear and respect mine."

Indeed, as I've heard it said, one of the strongest convictions you and I will ever have about ourselves is that we are right. Most surely we think we are right; otherwise we would change our minds. But

Barbara Spell

only God is always right. Therefore, I share in this book some of the wonders of what God says to women about what is good and right in marriage. After all, no one wants our marriages to thrive with love and joy more than the Lord Himself, who created marriage to reflect the love between Jesus Christ and His church. How can that happen?

Simply stated, marriage takes three. We need the Lord to teach us, and then we need Him to give us the willingness and power to step out in faith and do what He says. Otherwise, our well-meaning hearts will be unplugged from the power of love that gives life to our marriages. Trusting that third person—the Lord God Himself—is our power, our lifeline.

Two Ways to Live

There is an old song called, "Doin' What Comes Naturally." Thanks to being descendants of Adam, that is the way you and I were born— doing what comes naturally. The problem is that doing what comes naturally is usually not good—not good at all. Selfishness comes naturally. So does the desire to be in control and our refusal to forgive the ones who hurt us. Even the anger that comes when we don't get our way comes naturally. That's why one of my friends says, "If it comes naturally, we'd better think twice before we do it."

Fortunately there is another way to live. I call it doing what comes supernaturally—letting God do in and through us what we could never do by ourselves. That happens when He comes to us by His Spirit and gives us the grace to do the right thing, regardless of how we think or feel.

For instance, God says the wife is to respect her husband. But what if we believe our husbands are unworthy of our respect? Our natural response is to withhold it. We might cut them down with our words. Or we might pay little, if any, attention to them.

But God gives us a supernatural way to respond. His Spirit enables us to be kind and show respect despite how we think or feel. Many times when we are about to say something we shouldn't, the

Holy Spirit prompts us to be quiet. He can actually hold our words in check. I know that because of the many times He has stopped my mouth just in time!

One purpose of this book is to progressively move us from doing what comes naturally to doing what comes supernaturally through the presence and power of the Holy Spirit. But it is a major hurdle to get past our natural sense of self-sufficiency and acknowledge our need for God and His help. I devote chapter 8 to the subject of living by what comes naturally versus living by what comes supernaturally from the Spirit of God.

The Flight Attendant

A few years ago I was seated on a plane beside a twenty-six-year-old off-duty flight attendant. During our conversation she stated that although she wanted to marry, she was somewhat reluctant, knowing that the divorce rate is so high. She asked for any input that might encourage her. I talked to her about two things. First, that God needs to come first in a marriage. She remained silent. Second, we need to be willing to give up a degree of independence and control if we want an intimate relationship. She literally shuddered.

The words that followed were, "I don't think I can do that." In one sense, she was right. By herself she cannot. Living in the selfless commitment of marriage takes God's help. We talked more, and I can only hope our conversation made a positive and lasting impact.

I realize today's culture looks at marriage in a much looser way than when I married over fifty years ago. Casual and commitment-free relationships abound, and marriages end in divorce at staggering rates. There is a notable quest for independence among women that is greater now than when I was young. But even if you and I are cheerleaders for a certain amount of independence, don't we also want a close, intimate relationship with our husbands?

Here's the problem: to some extent, independence and intimacy are antithetical. It's hard to have it both ways. We might find ourselves taking charge and doing our own thing, but then we realize we don't have the closeness to our husbands that we yearn for.

I saw an amusing cartoon where two married ladies were having afternoon tea. One said to the other, "I'm afraid my desire for independence is getting in the way of my need for intimacy." Oh, what a lesson!

Some Things Never Change

Here's the sad fact: regardless of today's culture, from the beginning of time, neither man nor woman wanted anyone telling them what to do. Adam didn't. Eve didn't. We don't. And even though God is not just anyone, you and I (and our husbands) still have an inborn rebellious and independent streak that resists God. We simply prefer calling the shots ourselves. Meanwhile, cultures change. But God and His words do not.

I was amused when one of the ladies in our Bible study invited her grandmother to attend the class. The grandmother accepted the invitation quickly. But then she made a stunning statement. She said she would have to buy a new Bible because hers was old and she was sure it was out of date. One thing that dear lady knew was that the world is changing. What she did not know is that God and His Word are not.

As unstable as our world might appear, there is stability. But it is unseen. That stability is the truth and faithfulness of God and His word. "For I am the Lord, I do not change" (Malachi 3:6a). "Heaven and earth will pass away, but My words will by no means pass away" (Luke 21:33). God always means what He says. Listening to Him is safe ground.

My encouragement to you is to hear this out because what God tells us is life-giving. And as strange as it might seem, in the process of hearing what He says to wives, we realize we cannot willingly do anything He tells us to do without His help. And that is the beauty of this teaching. It takes us to a place of dependence upon God.

Accepting the proper concepts of helping, headship, submission, and respect does not and will not come naturally. It comes supernaturally—from the Spirit of God. And although we can obey unwillingly with clenched jaws, that is not what God is looking for. He wants us to have the peace that comes from trusting Him and His immeasurable love for us. He is ultimately drawing us to Himself. And that is good… really good.

Like Piano Notes

One day while playing the piano, it occurred to me that husbands and wives are something like piano notes. Individually played, each note produces a lovely sound. But when one note is united with a second note and they are played together, there is a new and more beautiful sound. Neither note loses its beauty when it is joined to another note. Instead the two notes produce a new and richer sound.

And there's more. When a third note is added, the sound becomes even richer. It becomes a threefold chord. Musically speaking, a chord is the combination of three or more tones sounded together in harmony. When played together, we hear just one new beautiful sound.

It made me think of something God says. Ecclesiastes 4:9–12 begins by stating that two are better than one—that people need companionship. The passage ends with those profound words, "And a threefold cord is not quickly broken." If we apply that to marriage, we see that when the third person is added to marriage, the relationship is at its strongest and least likely to break.

As an aside, it is interesting to twist together two pieces of cord and recognize how vulnerable they are to being frayed. But when a third piece of cord is braided in, I am told the bond is at its strongest. When you and I listen to what God says to us, and when we step out in faith and obey Him, we are engaging the almighty God—our strong cord—to hold our marriages together as he teaches us, directs us, and helps us experience His words, "a three-fold cord is not quickly broken." May these words of wisdom help us embrace the fact that marriage takes three: a husband, a wife, and our Creator, God.

A Mystery

Ephesians 5:31-32 states a profound truth: "For this reason a man shall leave his father and mother and be joined to his wife, and the two shall become one flesh. This is a great mystery, but I speak concerning Christ and the church." So God ordained marriage to be a visible, albeit finite, picture of the inseparable love between Jesus Christ and His bride, the church (the body of believers).

But how is marriage part of the mystery that points us to Christ? I believe the answer lies in this beautiful truth: In marriage, we can experience the most intimate knowledge and pleasure of another person. And that is how God wants us to know Him and His Son Jesus—personally, intimately, joyfully. Through the covenant of marriage, God offers us a glimpse of the love and intimacy the Lord Jesus wants you and me to have with Him.

The following thoughts help me understand what God is teaching us about the connection between our life as the bride of Christ and our life as the wife of our earthly husbands. First, as members of the church, we are betrothed to *Jesus*. We are being prepared for marriage to *Him*. We are not merely learning to be our husband's helper. Instead we are progressively learning the importance of being available to *Jesus* as His hands and feet on earth.

We are not being devalued by having our husbands named as "head of the wife." Instead we are progressively learning the importance of understanding authority and living under it as we look to *Jesus* as our head—our ultimate authority.

We are not being given a harsh order to submit to our husbands. Instead we are progressively learning the grace and beauty of a submissive heart as we look to *Jesus* and yield to Him and His will.

And finally, we are not being pushed into respecting our husbands unwillingly. Instead we are progressively learning to live by faith in God's words rather than by our feelings as we show respect, even reverence, to *Jesus*. Earthly marriage is more than meets the eye. It is about the love of Jesus for His bride, the church. We are deeply loved. Allowing that truth to sink in changes the way we live.

When I take a good look at my marriage, I realize the areas where I fall short as a wife are the same areas where I fall short with God. They invariably involve self-centeredness, control, or independence. I am so grateful for the patience and mercy of the Lord and my husband. I can't begin to count the times I have failed to give to either of them the time and attention they are due. Meanwhile, God's love for us remains steadfast.

One-sided Obedience

You and I might question whether it is worth learning and applying God's principles for marriage if our husbands are not doing what God tells *them* to do ("He's not loving me the way he should!"). Doesn't that make it useless for us to do what God tells *us*? It might seem so in the beginning, but obedience to God is never useless. We can trust Him. He often changes us before He changes our husbands. And even if our husbands never change the way we want them to, we can still have the joy of drawing closer to our heavenly Bridegroom, knowing we have honored Him with our obedience.

The good news is that we are responsible only for our own behavior and not for our husband's behavior. Our job is to follow what the Lord tells *us* to do and patiently pray for our husbands to know and apply what the Lord tells *them* to do. That is our peace, even amid troubling situations. Being a good wife is not dependent upon having a good husband. It is dependent upon following a good God. In fact, the exceptionable wife is exactly that—one who hears and follows the Lord Jesus.

Meanwhile, just as we thought our prince would never lose his charm, so did our husbands think their princess would never lose her allure. And so we and our prince entered marriage with the very best of intentions. But again, the stark reality is that we need help. God can bring back our allure. And He can bring back our husband's charm.

Summary

So why does marriage take three? Because good intentions can take us only so far. That rebellious, independent little streak in you and me pushes aside God's terms of marriage so we establish our own terms.

After more than fifty years of marriage, I can say without hesitation that God's ways prove perfect. His grace is always sufficient to help us do what is right. And when we fail, He understands and continues by His mercy to offer forgiveness, grace, and love. He is so patient with us.

> *My Son, give attention to My words ... For they are life*
> *to those who find them, and health to all their flesh.*
> *—Proverbs 4:20–22*

Dear Lord, even before I read this book, I thank You for understanding my natural tendency to resist learning and applying what You teach about the four difficult subjects of helper, headship, submission, and respect. I acknowledge I need help to embrace them. So please give me the grace to hear what you are trying to teach me. Please also teach my husband what You want him to learn so our marriage reflects a portion of the love and commitment that exists between You and Your church. Thank You. Amen.

Helper Needed

It is not good for the man to be alone.
I will make a helper suitable for him.
—Genesis 2:18 (NIV)

If you were asked to describe your relationship to your husband in one word, what would you say? After asking my sisters that question, one answered without hesitation, "I am his friend— his very best friend." The other sister smiled and said, "I am his lover." Both responses are beautiful. However, what impresses me is the one word God first used to describe a wife's relationship to her husband. She is to be his helper.

Of every word in the omniscient mind of almighty God, "helper" is the word He chose to describe the primary role of a wife. Would you or I have thought it? Or wanted it? Probably not because our natural mind thinks the role of a helper is inferior. But we are so wrong. He—the Lord Himself—is a helper.

Yes, God the Father, Jesus the Son, and the Holy Spirit are all referred to in the Bible as our helpers. Some of the ways a biblical helper can be defined are: an "aid," "assistant," "one who surrounds," "advocate," "comforter," "consoler," and "one who comes alongside." It is a magnificent role! It depicts the very nature of God.

A Profound Verse

In reading Genesis 2, we see that after God formed Adam, He placed him in a garden, gave him an assignment, and then made a statement that needs to be engraved on the heart of every wife: "It is not good for the man to be alone; I will make a helper suitable for him" (Genesis 2:18 NIV). What a profound declaration! Consider its uniqueness.

Who was there to hear those words except Adam? And God's words were not just addressed to Adam. It is as if God is thinking aloud and we get to listen as He prepares to create the first woman and initiate the first marriage. What an eye-opening privilege!

There are two parts of this revelation. May you and I never, ever separate them. The first part reveals a problem—a lonely man in need of companionship. The second part reveals God's remedy—the provision of a wife who will come alongside him as a helper. Sadly, the significance of this revelation often eludes us. Sometimes we simply don't see our husbands in need of our companionship or help. Nor do we see ourselves—or perhaps even want to see ourselves—as helpers. But regardless of how it seems, God created our husbands to need us.

Picture this: before woman was created, God brought to Adam the animals and birds He had created, and Adam named each one. But then God said something that always evokes a twinge of sadness in me: "But for Adam there was not found a helper suitable for him" (Genesis 2:20b NIV). Surrounded by the beautiful garden and a host of animals and birds, Adam was still lonely.

Although God had seen that everything was good after each day of creation, for the first time He said something was not good. What was not good? The man did not have his helper— someone who would be there for him. The man was in need. A woman, with all her gifts, strengths, sensitivities, and nurturing qualities, was the answer.

So God created a woman from the flesh and bones of the man. Adam gave her the name "woman," and God referred to her as Adam's wife. Clearly God chose to form man in need of a wife who would come alongside him in life as his helper. For me, this truth colors everything about my relationship to my husband. Even if it might seem otherwise, I know my husband needs me. And even if it might seem otherwise to you, your husband needs you too. And that is good.

Being Alone

Knowing that God said it is not good for the man to be alone, I asked my husband what it means to him not to be alone. He said simply, "Just to know you are on my side." What powerful words! It brings to mind something Jesus said: "He who is not with Me is against Me" (Matthew 12:30).

Your husband's response to the same question might be different, but I believe what my husband said is universally true. Unless we are on our husbands' side, they likely will feel lonely and distant from the one person they hoped would be their closest friend in life. How sad for a married man to feel alone. Unfortunately many wives also know the sorrow of loneliness.

As I began teaching this material, I asked my husband if he had ever felt alone during our marriage. After a while, he recalled an incident that occurred early in our marriage. We were driving down a mountain road a bit faster than usual when our young children in the back seat giggled and said, "Are you in a hurry or something, Dad?"

Instead of letting my husband respond, I quickly jumped in and agreed with the children. My husband said that at the time of the incident, he felt pretty much alone—three to one against him. By the way, the reason he was driving faster than usual (on the way to church of all things) was because I was running late. So it was not a good morning. Furthermore, siding publicly with children against their dad is not a good thing—morning, noon, or night.

A friend describes being on her husband's side as being on the same team with him. That way, when she thinks he is wrong, she still relates to him as a teammate, not an opponent. She remains his faithful companion even through disagreements.

Do we think of ourselves as being on the same team as our husbands? Marriage is not a competition calling for a winner. It is a union. Do we talk about *my* house and *my* children or about *our* house and *our* children? Do we usually say "*I* decided" or "*we* decided?" Our words reflect the way we think. God wants us to think of our marriages in terms of oneness, a union, a covenant commitment, of being on the same team.

Interestingly in Malachi 2:14b God refers to the wife as her husband's companion— a word whose root means "knit together." That is the opposite of "being alone." Ideally it means drawing close to our husbands not only physically, but emotionally and spiritually. Meanwhile, if our natural sense of selfishness and independence makes us resent the role of helper and companion, consider that it is God's call to knit us together with our husbands. And that's a worthy goal for every marriage.

Helping

When I consider the word "help" as meaning "to aid or to surround" (as Strong's Concordance defines it,) one word stands out to me. It is the word "surround." I like that word because it implies the person is present.

Quite by accident, I learned one place many husbands are alone is in their bed. I made a statement in the marriage class that my husband and I were in the habit of going to bed at the same time and that it was rare for us to bed down separately. That is easy for us because we both enjoy staying up late and are pretty much in sync on bedtime.

But what surprised me was the overwhelming response to my statement. Countless women, mostly young ones, told me they rarely go to bed when their husbands do. Either they are exhausted and need more sleep than their husbands do, or they consider the best time to get things done around the house is at night after everyone is in bed.

I understand both situations. Our sleep needs vary. My suggestion is that we and our husbands make some compromises occasionally and go to bed at the same time. There is something special about that quiet time when some of the cares of the world seem to have been lifted.

Therefore, whether it's enjoying sexual union or just enjoying the mutual satisfaction and companionship of lying next to one another in bed, isn't it good for our husbands to have us beside them at the end of the day? By habitually not joining them in bed, we might be unwittingly sending a message that something else is more important than they are. And if there is something more important to us, we need to talk to the Lord about it. He can change our hearts and habits in ways we cannot imagine.

An older woman told me her husband retired to the bedroom far too early for her. She was convinced he didn't care whether she joined him or not, so she stayed up long after he was asleep. One night she decided to change her habit and join him in his early bedtime. The next morning she called to say her husband responded to her presence in bed with a meaningful conversation. She was delighted and quite surprised.

Being Available

The fact is, being one who aids, helps, assists, and surrounds sounds easier than it might be. Why? Because it means we are available to them. We are there for them when they need us. What comes naturally is being so occupied with our own lives or our children's lives or our jobs, that sometimes we forget to leave room for our husbands. Since many wives have a full-time job, they and their husbands need to work out what is right and practical for them in acknowledging her role as a helper. Again, the point is that regardless of how it seems, God created our husbands to need us.

So how available are you and I to our husbands? Do we allow ourselves to be so busy that our husbands might see themselves as interruptions or as mere paychecks? In fact, do we even occasionally put our husbands "last"? Our husbands need to sense they are important to us. Frankly, they need to see us as their number-one fan.

Countless times you and I will face the choice of either "being there" for our husbands or going our own way. It could involve anything from joining them for a sporting event to simply being home with them. A newlywed friend told me how excited he had been about an upcoming hunting trip with friends and their wives.

But then his wife told him she really didn't have any interest in hunting and she had decided to stay home that weekend. Her decision resulted in a heartbroken husband who was both dejected and embarrassed by not having his newly-wed wife with him. It was a glowing sign to her husband that being with him was not as important to her as pursuing her own interests. They are now divorced.

Another newly-married friend told me that after she had spent much time on the computer one night, her husband gently approached her and asked if she were about through. He had been waiting alone for her much of the night.

Adapting

Several years ago I had the opportunity to speak to the wives of two respected Christian teachers. I asked them individually, "What one message would you send to young wives?" Surprisingly, their answers were identical: Learn to adapt! That was not an answer I expected. And I haven't seen those specific words in the Bible. Nevertheless, I think their answers are prudent and worth considering, so I include them. They involve walking alongside our husbands.

One wife said that had she known how many places they would live during their marriage, she might never have agreed to marry. She chuckled at the many ways she had adapted as her husband took her to places she never would have chosen for herself. She was clearly a joyous woman. The other wife said that had she not adapted to her husband's schedule, she would probably be divorced today. Instead she has had a full, fruitful life.

During my childhood, my dad's job caused our family to be transferred to a new location four times. I remember how much I hated leaving behind friends and memories as we moved to each new city. But as an adult, I now realize how hard these moves must have been for my mother. And yet I never heard her complain. Instead she would encourage my sisters and me into thinking we would love the next place more than the last. She assured us we would keep our current friends but make many new ones.

What my mother did, which I didn't recognize at the time, was adapt to each new situation, each new city, with a positive attitude. That doesn't mean moving was easy for her. It was surely a sacrifice. But she remained positive. What a source of help she must have been to my dad who likely had difficulty and even pain in uprooting our family so many times. How important to the family is a wife's attitude! In the event a move comes your way, ask God to help you adapt in such a way that your husband appreciates your "coming alongside" him.

An amusing, albeit seemingly trite, example of adapting occurred a few years ago. I told the marriage class about a friend who always greeted her husband at the end of the day with a tall glass of iced tea. Apparently the tea helped take the edge off his hectic day. So he would take the tea with him as he strolled to the bedroom and changed clothes.

A week or so later, a woman in class who was eager to be a model helper shared how she had tried the same thing for her husband. She excitedly greeted him at the end of the day with a tall glass of iced tea, waiting for his grand show of appreciation. But instead he looked at her with a puzzled face and asked in a bewildered fashion, "Why are you giving me tea? I don't drink tea!" In hindsight she laughed at her gaffe in copying the way one wife helped her husband unwind and trying to apply it to her own spouse. Our adapting must be to our own unique husband.

Barbara Spell

No Rules

What is beneficial or helpful to your husband or mine has no value to any woman except you and me. After fifty-plus years of marriage, I usually know what my husband wants or needs, whether it is quiet time to himself or the desire to have me nearby. For instance, there were periods of time when I knew my husband wanted me to be there (be physically present) after dinner, whether it involved talking, watching TV, or reading. What that meant for me was that I learned to do my piano playing, computer work, and telephone talking during the day. That situation might not apply to any wife except me because every marriage is unique and in its own season. The point is that it is good to be willing to adapt to situations that are helpful to our marriage.

Before my husband retired, he considered Friday nights special. After an intense week at the office, he looked forward to staying home where he could disengage from anything that took much thought or energy. As a result, off and on over the years we turned down invitations for Friday nights because my husband preferred to be home. At the time I probably was disappointed to decline invitations, and yet if I experienced disappointment, I don't remember it now. In hindsight, I realize I was adapting to his need for relaxation and building a closer relationship with him.

There is no list of rules to follow. Instead, the Lord leads and prompts us by His Spirit to do the right thing. Our job is to be sensitive to His promptings and then follow them. What our friends do or think should not prevent us from doing what is right for us. If it helps our husbands to spend quiet nights at home, let's be thankful they want to be home.

Comparing husbands and marriages is useless. Instead, God helps us adapt to our own unique husband. That doesn't negate the fact that our husbands will encounter many ways they need to adapt to our unique and perhaps peculiar ways and desires. Meanwhile let's not get that glass of iced tea ready for a man who doesn't drink tea.

Pleasing

One component of being a helper is rather unpopular yet important. It involves the word "pleasing." Actually, part of knowing God and growing closer to Him is learning what pleases Him and then doing it. Is it any different in marriage? The more we and our husbands know one another, the more we know what pleases and displeases each other. 1 Corinthians 7:33–34 says husbands and wives are to be concerned about how to please each other.

For me, that is a big part of being my husband's helper. I know what irritates him (not being somewhere on time), and I know what pleases him (being ready on time). Our challenge, of course, is to think about pleasing our husbands when we are far more inclined to think about ourselves and the ways we want them to please us. It most surely takes the good Lord to help us think right.

We do well to consider if there is something simple we can do that we know will please our husbands. If we are not working wives, it might be having meals at a reasonable time before they become irritated by an empty stomach. Or cooking something they love (a real gift since we eat out so often). And how pleasing it must be to be greeted by a smile. That might sound simplistic, but little gestures can become turning points in a marriage.

I remember a friend telling me about a particular evening when she and her husband were experiencing unusual tension in their marriage. She went to the grocery store, bought her husband's favorite candy bar, and then placed it on his pillow for later that night. When the time came, her husband spotted that candy bar and was so impressed by her simple gesture that he wrapped his arms around her. Tension dissolved. Amazing! My friend knew what would please her husband. *One little candy bar!*

Consider what Jesus said regarding His relationship to His Father: "The Father has not left me alone, for I always do those things that please Him" (John 8:29). What a remarkable statement! Let's ask God to give us the grace and insight to do those things that not only please Him, but those things that please our husbands. This is a tall order for every wife, and for the working wife, it is surely an even bigger challenge. But God knows every circumstance and longs to touch our hearts with this truth: our husbands need us.

"Whatever we ask we receive from Him (God) because we keep His commandments and do those things that are pleasing in His sight" (1 John 3:22). What a powerful promise relating to the obedience of pleasing!

Non-verbalized Needs

So do we think our husbands really need us? If the answer is "no," we need to discipline our minds to agree with God. He clearly says they do. But many, if not, most men don't "open up" as much as women do, so they likely need us in ways they never verbalize. What might those needs be? God knows what they are, so let's ask Him to show us.

Could your husband or mine be silently longing for our affirmation? Or our words of support and encouragement? Or simply our companionship? And when was the last time they received a compliment from us? Meanwhile, is the Lord silently waiting for us to intercede in prayer for them?

How much of a source of comfort and joy are you and I to our husbands? Are we helping make their lives easier or more difficult? Are we content with their provision, or are we pressuring them for more? When they are unduly stressed from their jobs, do we acknowledge it and offer something as simple as a back rub? Like us, our husbands need attention and encouragement.

My husband is a former fighter pilot. He has always wanted to own a plane. Well, we have celebrated our golden anniversary, and we still don't have a plane. Nevertheless, I will always help him keep his dream alive. Why would I discourage him? Why would I temper his hope with negativity? By God's grace I will come alongside him even in his dreams. Meanwhile he takes pleasure in reading his *Flying* magazines.

Summary

Although God would likely agree with my sisters that we are to be our own husband's best friend and lover, those weren't the words He first used to describe our role as wives. Being their helper is the way He defined our primary role. Our husbands were created with the need for a companion who would come alongside them in life as their best friend and helpmate. Our beloved Helper God is with us to make that possible. May He help us be sensitive to our husbands' needs—both spoken and unspoken. Like us, they want to be loved. Being a helper is a profound and serious role.

> *He who finds a wife finds a good thing,*
> *and obtains favor from the Lord.*
> *—Proverbs 18:22*

Dear Lord, thank You that I can call on You for help and that You hear and answer me. Please help me believe that my husband really needs me. Sometimes he seems so self-sufficient, or so distant. And many, if not most, times I don't feel needed, appreciated, or even interested. It's much easier to think of my own needs. But by Your grace, I will trust You and not my feelings that he really does need me.

Meanwhile, please help me think of ways to be the kind of helper he needs, and give me the desire to come alongside him so he knows he has a wife who is on his side in life and will be there for him. And then please open his heart to see in me a helper whom he needs and cherishes. Thank You, dear Lord. Amen.

Helper Available

I will lift up my eyes to the hills. From whence comes my help?
My help comes from the Lord, Who made heaven and earth.
—Psalm 121:1–2

Our Help: God!

Oh, how wise is our God! He created husbands to need a helpmate. And He created wives to be that helpmate. But something happened. Adam disobeyed God. Thereafter, every descendant of Adam was born with his nature—self-centered and rebellious. So the husband needs a helper, but the wife doesn't want to be that helper. And therein lies the wisdom of God. He knows that without His help, we are incapable of willingly doing anything He calls us to do. Out of pure love, the almighty Helper is drawing us to Himself—to know and depend upon Him and His help. And that is indeed good.

As mentioned previously, God the Father, the Son, and the Holy Spirit are all referred to as helpers. Some versions of the Bible use the words "comforter" or "counselor" in place of "helper." The word means "advocate, comforter, consoler, intercessor, and one who comes alongside to help." That is the very nature of God—a helper! He who created us in His image to reflect what He is like is slowly transforming us to become more and more like Him, the magnificent Helper. In fact, every gesture of help and comfort that we offer our husbands displays the very nature of God. May we never underestimate the role of helper. It is a beautiful, serious, and very high calling.

How serious and beautiful is God's role as a helper? For me it has been a matter of life and death. In fact, I weep with tears of gratitude when I consider the numerous times God has answered my calls to Him for help. There have been a few desperate situations in which I have literally cried out, "Jesus, please help us!" I mean, I have really cried out. I will never forget the night my husband fell in the bathroom of a hotel in California. I was awakened by the noise of the toilet tank lid rattling and a loud thud. My husband was on the floor, partially under the dressing table and wasn't moving. I belted out cries to Jesus for help. I didn't whisper. I cried out repeatedly and loudly. After what seemed like at least five minutes, he opened his eyes. The Helper had heard and answered my cries.

But even more dramatic cries for God's help came thirty-four years ago during a Sunday morning church service. Suddenly, my husband slumped forward, hitting his head hard on the pew in front of us. He was motionless. His heavy body was lifted onto the pew where he laid, still motionless. The whole church prayed. And prayed. Minutes passed. He continued to look lifeless for what seemed like an eternity. And then in that precious moment of time, his eyes opened.

Applause and joy filled the church. Paramedics on the scene said all signs were normal. A doctor's appointment the next day and subsequent tests revealed all was normal. The doctor told us he was sorry, but he had no explanation for what happened. God alone knows. How I praise Him! I believe my husband and I are living testimonies that "Unless the Lord had given me help, I would soon have dwelt in the silence of death" (Psalm 94:17 NIV). Oh how magnificent is our helper God!

Being a Helper

When I first embraced the importance of the role of a helper, I asked my husband how I could best be of help to him. He gently answered,

"Just do the things I ask." Fortunately for me, my husband doesn't make unreasonable requests. If yours does, your response will be to consider what is truly reasonable and do it. That, of course, is a subjective matter.

My husband is quiet and easygoing. What I have learned is that even with a lovable husband, being available to help him remains a choice, albeit an easier one. As the wife of a good-natured husband, I have to guard against taking advantage of him. If I didn't respond to his requests or need for help, it is unlikely he would raise his voice or show much anger. On the surface, I might get by with ignoring his requests, but I would have missed the mark. And there would be a silent weakening of our relationship.

You and I do well to consider if there is something we are doing (or not doing) that might be causing a silent weakening of our relationship with our husbands. God can bring whatever it is to our minds if we ask Him.

My husband's request that I just do the things he asks reminded me of the wedding in Cana when the supply of wine ran out. In response to that disturbing situation, Jesus's mother told the servants, "Whatever He (Jesus) says to you, do it" (John 2:1–11). The servants did as Jesus said, filling the waterpots with water, and the water miraculously became wine.

That wine was evidence of the life, joy, and transforming power that is released when we listen to Jesus and do what He says. He knows how to make things new. That includes marriage relationships. Could a similar transformation take place in our marriages if we would listen more carefully to our husbands and follow through on what they ask us to do?

Ask Him

Consider asking your husband how you can best be a helper to him. That is a risky question to ask, so be prepared for an unexpected answer. It is especially risky and difficult for a working wife who comes home ready to be helped, not to help. But let's consider the significance of the role of a helper and then talk to the Lord about our concerns. He knows everything about our circumstances and future. He can show us how to be the kind of helper our own unique husband needs.

When the women in the marriage class asked their husbands how they could be of help, some were astounded by the answers. Most women thought their husbands wouldn't have much to say, but they learned differently. A few women were asked to take over the family's bookkeeping. For one, it meant learning how to use a new computer program. Another woman was simply asked to keep the old-fashioned checkbook balanced. That's when she reported with laughter that her husband had been right all along—They really did *not* have any money!

Especially surprised was the wife whose husband asked her to help him part-time at the office. She complied and was struck by how much help he needed and how rewarding it was to help him. Many women said they thought their husbands really didn't want or need their help. But then they asked. That was when they learned differently. Sometimes it was a serious request. Other times, it was light-hearted.

For instance, one wife asked her husband as he was leaving for work, "Is there anything I can do for you today?" She said he seemed startled by the question and quickly said "no" as he left for work. But then something happened. The phone rang. It was her husband saying, "You asked if there were something you could do for me today. Well, yes, I sure would like to get the dog washed."

She was not thrilled with his request. But she washed the dog. That evening when her husband came home, she knew she had done the right thing because among his first words to her were, "Did the dog get his bath?" He was delighted because dog-bath time was usually his job.

These examples might seem unimportant or trivial, but are they? Only God knows the extent of how being a helper to our husbands nourishes and cultivates a closer relationship with them.

If you are not a working wife, consider asking your husband as he leaves for work each morning if there is anything you can do for him that day. Untold blessings can be reaped from that one simple offering. His request might be as simple as picking up the laundry or even as easy as my husband's first request, which was almost too easy to repeat. He simply said he was about out of toothpaste. So I bought toothpaste. Following through on even a tiny request is important because God says, "He who is faithful in what is least is faithful also in much …" (Luke 16:10).

Even if we get no requests, our words will have registered with our husbands that we were thinking of them. And that is good. So the responses will vary, but the principle is the same. Being available to our husbands reflects being available to the Lord, our heavenly Bridegroom.

The Praying Helper

There is both visible and invisible help. No one but God knows the full impact of a praying wife. I will never forget a man sharing his story of being depressed and ready to give up his ministry. He said when he went to bed one night, he was prepared to call it quits the following day. However, upon awakening he was refreshed and eager to continue. He then learned his wife had been up much of the night praying for him. After that, his ministry continued and thrived.

How much of our day or night is given to prayer for our husbands? In addition to our private prayers, we might also consider praying out loud for them when we lie beside them in bed. The habit my husband and I have of praying together each night began by simply praying the Lord's Prayer out loud together.

If you and your husband don't now pray together, you might ask him one night in bed if there is anything he would like for you to pray for him. But be prepared for a negative response because prayer is a touchy subject and your husband might flat-out refuse. If he does, accept that refusal without being offended. On the other hand, you might get a surprisingly positive response. In fact, it might be the biggest boost he's had in a long time.

Help is not meant to be one-sided. So if we are concerned because of our great need for our husband's help, we need to talk to them about it. Instead of harboring resentment, we do well to tell them exactly what we need. But our words need to be careful and gracious so we don't put them on the defensive.

Also we can and should express to God our need for *His* help. God has assured us He knows what we need even before we ask, but we are still to ask Him. He knows the exact kind of help working women and mothers of small children need. He knows the husbands who fail to share in household responsibilities. So if our husbands define our requests for their help as "nagging," we do well to leave those requests in God's hands. He can be trusted to give us the help and strength we need. We, too, need a helper. And He is available—always.

Being Sensitive

It is important to develop a sensitivity to the presence of the Holy Spirit. He will convict us of specific ways to reach out to our husbands when they need our help. Whether it is a physical, emotional, or spiritual need, they need us. When they are sick or in pain, they need our comfort. When they are experiencing disappointment or failure, they need our encouragement and affirmation. When they are hurting or worrying, they need our support and prayer. They might also need us to wrap our arms around them, cry or laugh with them, or maybe just listen to them and be there for them. There is a God-given capacity for comforting and nurturing that women possess. Let's be sure our husbands receive that comfort, affirmation, encouragement, and support from us and not some other woman.

Before my husband retired, he occasionally traveled. On each occasion, I tucked a little poem or note inside his luggage. Each one said the same thing in a different way—that I loved him and was thinking of him. You know what? A few years ago I discovered that not one of those notes has ever been discarded. I had opened a piece of luggage that I seldom used, and there they were—a collection of three-by-five cards. He had kept every one.

Our husbands need us. If we think otherwise, we are wrong. What we must grasp is that our husbands need faithful companions—ones who will affirm and encourage them and make peaceful homes for them—not critics or independent housemates. Numerous women have criticized or neglected their husbands for years, having taken them for granted while carving out their own lives. Sometime later many of them want a relationship that has long since evaporated. So their response is, "He doesn't need me."

Fortunately, it is never too late to turn our behavior around (to repent), and often it is not too late to bring life back to a weak marriage. If we can identify with being critical, independent wives, we can humble ourselves by acknowledging our sins and asking the Lord for a new start. Perhaps we will be able to write the same note to our husbands that a friend wrote to hers: "I needed you! ... but then I realized you needed me."

After fifty-plus years of marriage, I can think of no instance where my fault-finding or efforts to instruct my husband benefited him. Instead, what has benefited him is each and every word of encouragement. You and I were created to help our husbands, not to criticize, teach, judge, nag, or mother them. Most emphatically, we are not their Holy Spirit.

I am reminded of a young woman who asked the Lord to show her how to be a better wife. She got her answer one night shortly thereafter when her husband unexpectedly blurted out, "I'm tired of being mothered. I just want a wife."

I also recall an unhappily married man telling my husband and me that after many years of marriage, his wife was still trying to teach him. He said she never "got it" that he was out of school and simply wanted a wife.

We are all looking for the same thing in life—someone who really cares about us and loves and accepts us with all our imperfections.

Even if we don't get praise from our husbands when we care for them, we have pleased God, and that is good—very good.

Keep in mind that a situation might arise where we cannot give our husbands the attention we would otherwise give. It could be our parents, another family member, or even you or I who might have a season of special need (like illness) that takes our time and energy away from our husbands. In that case, we can at least acknowledge to them that our lack of attention is unrelated to our love for them. They need to know how much we care about them. Isn't that what you and I also want—a husband who really cares about us?

Summary

In His infinite love for us, the Lord chose to welcome His bride (the church), to come alongside Him to serve Him as His earthly helper. How? We are His hands and feet on this earth, sent to serve, preach the gospel, and pray. He said whatever we do to the least of His brethren, we do to Him (Matthew 25:40).

The time we spend alone with the Lord each day is the most important time of the day. Yet what comes naturally is letting the cares of this world keep us from being available to Jesus—serving, enjoying, and being a source of pleasure to Him.

Is it any different in marriage? Instead of being available to serve, enjoy, and be a source of pleasure to each other, we and our husbands might unintentionally neglect each other. I've often thought that the kind of life a husband experiences on this earth can be the result of the kind of wife he has (and vice versa). It is a sobering thought. How can we and our husbands be a source of joy or peace or any kind of help to each other if we are unavailable and wrapped up in our own world?

Much of our culture is geared toward individuality and independence. We need to discipline ourselves (make the decision) to reject those tendencies. Blessing comes in obedience to God, not in conformity to the ways of the world. The world might laugh at the suggestion that we set our hearts to be our husband's helper. The world might laugh that we aim to let our husbands know they are loved and important to us. But 1 John 2:15–17 tells us that the things of this world are not from God.

The woman who goes against the ways of the world by embracing the role of helper is a beautiful example of what it means to be an exceptional wife. According to the Random House Dictionary, that means she is "unusual; extraordinary; unusually excellent; superior; gifted; uncommon; peculiar; and rare." Beautiful indeed!

Surely there are needs only God can supply, but He created our husbands with needs only we as their wives can meet. It brings to mind the succinct words of wisdom given to a young friend by her mother-in-law: "Husbands need lots of 'tendin." Let's be sure it is we who tend to them. After all, do we want another woman to give our husbands the "tending to" that they aren't getting from us?

When we receive Jesus in our lives, we don't have to do what comes naturally and tend more to ourselves than to our husbands. We don't have to resent being a helper. We are united with Jesus— the greatest Helper of all. His life flowing through us gives us the desire and ability to come alongside our husbands as their reliable helpers. That is doing what comes supernaturally. That is loving and cherishing our husbands as we promised.

> *Behold, God is my helper …*
> *—Psalm 54:4*

Dear Lord, thank You that even with all my frustrations, I can always depend upon You to be with me as my personal Helper. Please help me know what my husband needs from me. And then please give me the desire and strength to meet those needs. Even if I receive no appreciation from him when I help him, I trust You will give me joy in knowing I am pleasing You. Also please give my husband a sensitivity to *my* needs and a willingness to help me when I need *his* help. Thank You. Amen.

In The Garden: What's To Eat?

*A good wife ... does her husband good, and
not harm, all the days of her life.*
—*Proverbs 31:10, 12 (RSV)*

From time to time we hear about a marriage that's in trouble, and we are stunned. My husband and I experienced that early in our marriage. A jovial couple in our dinner club was the delight of every dinner, full of laughter and the picture of happiness. Then in a moment that shocked us all, the husband filed for divorce. What appeared blissful on the outside completely masked the true nature of the relationship that existed behind closed doors.

In Genesis 2–3, God gives us a gift of inestimable value. He takes us "behind the doors" of the first marriage to let us witness the events that led to the breakdown in relationships. Here in the garden of Eden, our eyes are opened. We see the beginning of marriage, the beginning of trouble in marriage, the beginning of temptation, the beginning of man's sin, and the beginning of man experiencing God's provision for sin. We see the roots of all marital problems being exposed and every principle addressed in this book being violated. We observe how the first husband fared in his role as head of his wife and how the first wife fared in her role as her husband's helper. In a word, we see ourselves.

If you and I ever wonder why it is difficult to follow through on our good intentions in marriage, these chapters show us why. We are descendants of Adam, and we inherited his nature— a nature that always rebels against God and operates independently of Him. Until we look to God as our "boss" for guidance and help, that rebellious, independent nature is our boss. Fortunately, when we receive Jesus in our lives, He gives us a new nature that is able to behave differently. But being able to behave differently doesn't mean we always do. It means we have the power through the Holy Spirit to do the right thing.

The Original Declaration of Independence

Unfolding before us in Genesis 2–3 is a picture of the futility of a man and a woman trying to live their lives independent of God. Adam, the first man created on earth, ignored and thereby rejected the authority of God and His words. How? He ate the fruit God told him not to eat. Eve, the first woman created, ignored and thereby rejected the authority of her husband and his words that were spoken to him by God. How? She also ate the forbidden fruit. Result: the original Declaration of Independence was authored in the garden of Eden. Why, oh why, do we presume we can go it alone?

Have you and I ever considered what the ultimate independence in marriage would be? It would be either divorce or death. So do we really want our independence? I once asked a divorced friend if she would ever consider marrying again. She laughed and said, "Oh no, I'm far too independent for that." Sadly in her loneliness, she now drinks herself to sleep at night.

God made us to be dependent upon Him. And He created husbands and wives to be interdependent. Did He really say that? Yes, in 1 Corinthians 11:11—12. That truth might be hard to swallow, but the fact is that God made our husbands to need us. He also made us to need our husbands. And that is good.

Adam: Given Responsibility and Headship

Let's observe Adam, the world's first husband. After God formed Adam, He planted a garden, placed Adam in it, and gave him a specific job to do. The Lord God "took the man and put him in the garden of Eden to tend and keep it" (Genesis 2:15). The word "keep" in this passage means to guard, protect, and attend to. There is Adam's assignment—to take care of the garden. It sounds simple enough.

God then permitted Adam to eat freely from every tree in the garden except one—the Tree of the Knowledge of Good and Evil. God followed that prohibition by warning him that the consequence of eating from that one tree would be, "you shall surely die" (Genesis 2:17). Adam's job just became less simple. He was given a restriction. And who wants restrictions, even when they are given to us for our own good?

Mercifully, God tells us what is and is not good to do. He didn't create us and then leave us to fend for ourselves. Instead, He instructs us in the knowledge of what is good and what is evil. Thus, we can learn either by instruction or experience. Following instruction is easier, but our nature is not to let someone tell us what to do, so we just go experience for ourselves that we should have listened to God all along. Marriage will teach us that over and over.

Often God gives us promises that follow obedience and warnings that follow disobedience. Then He gives us a choice. In this case, Adam had the choice to eat or not eat from the prohibited tree. The warning was death. Adam knew what he was not to eat. Surely he would honor that one crucial restriction.

Now that God gave Adam His instruction, He gave him something else— the gift of a wife, a helper. Adam then had the responsibility to tell Eve what was and was not permissible to eat. The implication is that Adam told her. She would never need to ask, "What can we eat?" because she, too, would know.

The newlyweds were set to walk as one and live happily ever after. Adam would take care of both the garden and his wife, and Eve would come alongside him, cooperating with him as his invaluable helper. They would both exercise God-given authority over creation. And neither of them would ever eat from the Tree of the Knowledge of Good and Evil ... or so it could have been.

Company Arrives

Suddenly, the peaceful honeymoon was interrupted by the arrival of unexpected company. A serpent appeared in the garden. "Now the serpent was more cunning than any beast of the field which the Lord God had made ..." (Genesis 3:1). We don't know what the serpent looked like or where he came from. What we do know is that God gave Adam authority to name every beast of the field. And there is a connection between a name and the character it represents. So if the serpent were one of the creatures Adam named, one would think Adam knew it was a crafty being. And if the serpent were not a creature Adam had named, one wonders if Adam should have been all the more wary of this strange creature. Regardless, the serpent was in the garden long enough to do his job.

Serpent Heads for Eve

Who is this serpent? He is "that serpent of old, called the Devil and Satan, who deceives the whole world" (Revelation 12:9). His fate is to end up in the lake of fire and brimstone where he will be tormented day and night forever (Revelation 20:10). But for now, he is making his first appearance before the human race. And to whom does that deceiving devil go? He heads straight for the woman.

The time has come for this crafty serpent to activate his plan of deception. He would say just enough to draw Eve and then Adam away from their dependence upon God and the reliability of His words. So he asks Eve the famous question, "Has God indeed said, 'You shall not eat of every tree of the garden'?"(Genesis 3:1). This is his first injection of the poisonous words of temptation that cause Eve to doubt God's word. Implicit in this question is the suggestion that God is withholding something good from her (and Adam.) And who wants to be denied anything?

Consider what a vivid picture God shows us of one way Satan works. He works to move our focus away from enjoying and thanking God for all He has given us. In this case, Adam and Eve were given the fruit from every tree except one. But Satan tempts us to focus on that which we cannot or do not have. Could that happen to us today in our marriages?

Oh, how we need to beware of the temptation before us to yearn for more without being grateful for what we already have. Rather than focusing on what we don't have, our whole perspective changes when we become grateful for what we do have—every day. We have the Lord, along with His love, forgiveness, presence, mercy, and promise of everlasting life in heaven in Christ. And on the physical side of life, are we thankful for our children, family, home, church, friends, and more? Or are we looking at that one thing we have been denied?

Eve Entertains Company

So what was Eve to do? Let's put ourselves in her shoes. How would you and I respond if we were in Eve's situation? Do you and I sometimes engage in conversations we should leave alone, perhaps because we are not strong enough in our knowledge or faith to respond wisely? Or because we are likely to say too much? Or because it is an area of expertise in which we feel eminently qualified to comment? Or more likely still, because the answer should come from our husbands?

It's so good to know when to remain silent. There is a time to be quiet and a time to speak. The Holy Spirit knows the time. And He knows how to nudge us when we're about to say too much or too little. After years of letting my tongue get carried away, I am slowly learning to sense God's nudging before my tongue spews out trouble or I answer a question that was directed to my husband.

Remarkably, Eve didn't refer the serpent to Adam. After all, the serpent was questioning her about what God had told her husband. Instead, Eve entertained the serpent's words and "took him on" herself. Can we not identify with that? Are there are situations we are trying to deal with that are meant for our husbands—or situations where we should consult our husbands? Eve gives new meaning to the expression of being "in over my head." She was trusting in her own ability and wisdom rather than in God's or Adam's words. Do we not have that same tendency toward pride—faith in ourselves and our good judgment?

So Eve conversed with the serpent, explaining that they could eat the fruit of the trees of the garden but could neither eat nor touch the fruit from one particular tree or they would die. The word "touch" was an exaggeration. Nevertheless, Eve clearly knew what was not to eat. Adam's words should have been uppermost in her mind, especially because the life-or-death warning had come to Adam from God. But Eve responded independently of her husband, and deception awaited her.

Once Eve entered into a conversation with the serpent, he had a "field day" by directly contradicting God's words with the lie, "You will not surely die. For God knows that in the day you eat of it your eyes will be opened, and you will be like God, knowing good and evil" (Genesis 3:4–11). In one sense, it is not wrong to want to be like God and have knowledge, but it is wrong to think we can be like God and have knowledge without depending upon Him and His words.

So Eve allowed her own sense of good and evil to eclipse the God-given words Adam spoke to her. She let the lust of the flesh (the fruit would taste delicious), the lust of the eyes (it looked beautiful), and the pride of life (she would be like God, knowing good and evil) entice her to eat. "For all that is in the world—the lust of the flesh, the lust of the eyes, and the pride of life—is not of the Father but is of the world" (1 John 2:16). Based on this story in the garden, I have heard it suggested that the primary weakness of a woman is her tendency to trust her own wisdom, her own judgment.

How likely are we to do the same? How often do we come down from the supernatural world of trusting God to the natural world of trusting ourselves, our wisdom, and our senses? Things are not always as they appear. When we watch the sun set behind the earth's horizon, it's hard to believe the sun isn't moving. But we know the earth is moving, not the sun. Our senses can betray us. Satan makes himself look like an angel of light (2 Corinthians 11:14). So might the man who wants to tempt you or me to betray our commitment to our husbands. He, too, knows how to attract and entice.

Attractive Poison

Sin is deceitful. It might look good, but it is poison wrapped in a beautiful container. Attractive poison surrounds us. I know a woman who was enjoying her clandestine affair. Her words to me were, "But my husband is so distant and disinterested, and this man is so attentive and good to me." That is attractive poison. What man wouldn't be attentive to a woman he wants to lure into the bedroom?

So, relying on her senses and anticipating the pleasure, Eve drew near to the attractive poison. She "took of its fruit and ate…" The first woman on earth just rationalized her way into disobedience. It started when she listened to the wrong voice—the poisonous voice of the serpent—and entertained doubt in God's word. Thus, "Eve was deceived by the serpent's cunning…" (2 Corinthians 11:3 NIV).

Whatever became of Adam's words to avoid eating from that one tree? How dramatically Eve's story depicts the ease with which we can disregard what God or our husbands say and instead trust ourselves.

Adam: Renegade Leader and Protector

After Eve bit into the fruit, "she also gave to her husband with her, and he ate" (Genesis 3:6). Two words stand out: "with her." We don't know how long Adam had been standing beside Eve before she "took of its fruit," but we do know he was there in time to stop her. Not only could he have prevented her from eating it, but he knew God said eating fruit from that particular tree would bring death.

Where was the responsible and protective husband? Adam simply disregarded God's words, and he didn't protect Eve. Could he not have intervened before she ate?

The next two words are the reason Adam is held responsible for the fall of the entire human race: "he ate" (Genesis 3:6). God says when we know the right thing to do and we don't do it, it is sin (James 4:17). Adam knew. Whereas Eve was deceived, Adam was not.

So here before us is the origin of sin, the fall of man, and the first role reversal in the universe. Adam directly disobeyed God by accepting his wife's offer to eat the forbidden fruit rather than obeying God's words not to eat. Eve indirectly disobeyed God by ignoring her husband's God-given words of instruction not to eat, and therefore she ate and enticed him to eat. And there began a pattern that persists to this day: the wife initiates; the husband responds. She leads; he follows. It brings with it untold damage to marriages.

Sin "Stings"

When Adam followed Eve in eating the forbidden fruit, he experienced the death about which God had forewarned. That death would now be passed on to the entire human race. "The sting of death is sin…" (1 Corinthians 15:56). Like a bee stinging a person and injecting fatal poison, sin became the poison that brought death to every man—immediate spiritual death and eventual physical death.

That is the disaster that results when we as God's little creatures detach ourselves from our mighty Creator and think we can function without Him and His life-giving words. It is also a picture of the first wife detaching herself from her husband by ignoring his words of direction. Some might say the term "dysfunctional" was birthed here in the garden of Eden. The sober reality is that the serpent got to Adam through his wife. Are we naïve enough to think he has changed his tactics?

The Tempter Still Speaks

The drama in the garden of Eden continues to be of utmost relevance. The following is an example of how it might be played out in our lives today. Satan has not changed. He is still the deceiving tempter who wants us to question God's word and renege on our promise to love and cherish our husbands. His sly voice might sound something like this (Barbara Spell's paraphrase):

> Now the serpent was more cunning than any beast of the field which the Lord +God had made (Genesis 3:1). And he asked the woman if God indeed said she was to be her husband's helper. The woman answered the serpent by telling him that yes, indeed, God said it isn't good for the man to be by himself, so He made her to be his helper. Then the serpent told the woman that she certainly was not made for her husband … that her husband lives in his own little world and gets along fine without her. In fact, he doesn't even notice when she helps him. What she needs to do is help **others** who appreciate her.
>
> So when the woman acknowledged that she did not get many thanks around the house, and that she was the one who needed a helper, and that it was she who was lonely, she decided to carve out a world of her own. And then she and her husband went their own separate ways …

"A good wife who can find? … She does him (her husband) good, and not harm, all the days of her life" (Proverbs 31:10, 12 RSV). Eve was the gift God created for Adam to be his helper. Yet she did him devastating harm when she allowed the voice of a strange serpent to have more impact than the voice of her own husband. What an on-going warning God has given you and me.

> *My son, give attention to my words … Keep them*
> *in the midst of your heart; For they are life to those*
> *who find them, And health to all their flesh.*
> *—Proverbs 4:20–22*

Dear Lord, please help me learn from Eve's mistakes—especially that I give more weight to my husband's words. Show me where I am relying on my own senses rather than asking the Holy Spirit to show me what is good and right and true. Also, please guard me against deceit. If anyone tempts me with enticing words that contradict your words, help me recognize those words as attractive poison which You will help me reject. Please also help my husband be more responsible in taking care of me and our family. Thank You. Amen.

In the Garden: Food Poisoning

There is a way that seems right to a man,
But its end is the way of death.
—Proverbs 14:12

I have heard of rocky honeymoons, but nothing compares to the thorny problems that surfaced during the first honeymoon in the garden of Eden. As soon as Adam and Eve ate the forbidden fruit, their peaceful honeymoon came to an abrupt halt. Both suffered severe food poisoning. The fruit that was perfect on the tree became poisonous to their systems when they ate it in disobedience. They had filled themselves with sin. Although God offered them food from every tree in the garden except one, they chose to eat from that one forbidden tree. Let's put ourselves in the garden for a minute and see how the choices Adam and Eve made look all too familiar.

Beauty and the Beast: Two Voices

Beauty and the Beast is a story much older than what is written in a book or produced in a play. The real (original) story began in the garden of Eden where two opposing voices spoke. First came the voice of Beauty. God, who is pure Beauty (Psalm 27:4), spoke truth and life to Adam and Eve. The Beast, a serpent called a "beast of the field," spoke lies that brought death. This serpent was not the usual beast of the field for whom God cares (Psalm 50:10–11). He was the wild, evil, and very real beast of Revelation 12:9 who is God's enemy, seeking to be worshipped. He is capable of disguising himself so he appears beautiful. But he speaks poison.

And it is here in the garden that we hear for the first time two conflicting voices. Adam first heard God say not to eat from one particular tree. But later he heard Eve's voice offer him delicious fruit from that same tree. Meanwhile, Eve heard Adam say they were not to eat from that one particular tree. But later she heard the serpent say it was all right to eat from that same tree. Conflicting voices are something you and I will hear for our entire lives. What's the result? Adam and Eve each followed the wrong voice. As a teacher of mine often taught, the voice we follow determines the direction of our lives. That truth cannot be overemphasized.

I am reminded of a woman who was confronted with two opposing voices. She was stunned one day to learn her husband whom she loved was having an affair. She shared her devastating news with two close friends. But her friends had different responses. One friend advised her to lock her husband out of the house and seek a divorce lawyer. This friend knew adultery was legitimate grounds for divorce since it breaks the marriage covenant. So divorce was her quick advice.

A second friend advised her to immerse herself in prayer and to treat her husband with kindness and grace, forgiving him and praying for him to have a change of heart. She weighed both voices. She decided to follow the voice that offered forgiveness and hope. Only a few days later, her husband approached her with tears of sorrow for hurting her so deeply and asked for forgiveness. In time, their marriage thrived. She had listened to the right voice.

Naked! Then Clothed!

Where did this failure to heed the right voice leave Adam and Eve? Naked. Their eyes were opened, and they realized they were naked. So they sewed fig leaves together and hid themselves from God (or so they thought). But God spoke and asked Adam where he was. That's when Adam told God that he was afraid because he was naked, so he hid himself.

That sense of nakedness is a picture of the realization of their sin, which they wanted to cover and then quickly hide. They knew they were not right with God. Were it not so tragic, it would be amusing to realize how desperately we try to cover our sins and not be exposed. Instead of confessing our rebellion against God and having peace, we become masters of the cover-up. If there is something you or I are keeping covered, we do well to spill it out before the Lord and receive His gracious forgiveness and peace.

The good news is that God provided a covering for Adam and Eve that made them acceptable to Him. How? He clothed them (covered them) with garments made from animal skin, meaning an animal was killed in their place. They didn't keel over and die for their rebellion against God. Instead, an animal died in their place. That animal sacrifice pointed toward the sacrifice of Jesus, who would pay the price for the sins of the world.

Today you and I can thank God that we, too, are made acceptable to Him because the Lamb of God, Jesus, has been sacrificed in our place. We are now actually clothed with garments of salvation and invisible robes of righteousness. What a gift—being made right with God through the sacrifice of Jesus Christ (Genesis 3:21; Isaiah 61:10).

Regardless of how far you and I fall short of our good intentions in marriage, we can be assured we are forgiven through Jesus. He is the only antidote for the food poisoning that affects all men everywhere, for He alone takes away our sin. We will fall short again and again, but with love and forgiveness in His hands, He is always with us to pick us up.

Think Consequentially

Years ago I heard a sermon entitled, "Think Consequentially." That is, we need to think of the consequence of our behavior before we speak or act. Adam and Eve needed that message. Their disobedience was costly not only to them, but to every one of their descendants. And so it is for us. The way we live affects our beloved children. Be aware that the beautifully-wrapped Beast will make many overtures in our marriages and tempt us with much attractive poison—from dishonesty to infidelity. When tempted, think consequentially. The Holy Spirit gives us the strength to say no. The following are two unpleasant consequences of Adam and Eve's sin that continue to affect you and me today.

Consequence #1: Increased Pain in Childbirth

The food poisoning suffered by Adam and Eve when they ate the forbidden fruit was accompanied by pain that did not decrease the next day or the next. It would continue throughout all generations.

"To the woman He said: 'I will greatly increase your pains in childbearing; with pain you will give birth to children. Your desire will be for your husband, and he will rule over you'" (Genesis 3:16 NIV). There are two parts to this pronouncement, one concerning children and the other concerning husbands. I believe both relate to the issue of authority.

Regarding the part about children, I offer my personal thoughts. As a mother, I know childbearing can be painful, but my question has always been why this increased pain was a part of the consequence of Eve's behavior. Logic tells me that because God is perfect and just, this consequence was related to either what Eve did or what she failed to do. So what did Eve do or fail to do? What she did was listen to and follow the serpent's words. What she did not do was listen to and follow her husband's words (which God had spoken to him). In other words, she gave more authority to the serpent's voice than to her husband's voice. And the voice we follow indicates who has authority in our lives.

How would the issue of authority apply here? How would it translate into increased pain in childbearing? Where is a woman's authority in the home? It is as a parent to her children. From the beginning of time, God established the authority structure for the husband and wife (husband is the head of the wife) as well as for the parent and child. Children are to obey their parents (Ephesians 6:1).

Eve failed in the area of staying under the proper authority. She by-passed Adam's words and chose to eat the fruit. In effect, she rebelled against his authority. I believe it is reasonable to say the consequence Eve and her offspring would reap is the painful suffering of giving birth to children over whom they will have authority. In other words, reproducing another little rebel would now be with increased pain.

Consequence #2: Woman's "Desire"

The second part of the Genesis 3:16 verse is vital to grasp: "Your desire shall be for your husband, and he shall rule over you." Although respectable teachers differ on their understanding of the word "desire" in this passage, I offer what I believe is the most accepted and probable interpretation in the context of pronouncing judgment.

There are only three places in the Bible where the word "desire" has the same root meaning: Genesis 3:16, Genesis 4:7, and Song of Solomon 7:10. In Genesis 3:16, God tells Eve that she will now have a desire for her husband and he shall rule over her. In Genesis 4:7, God tells Cain that sin lies at the door and its desire is for him, but he should rule over it. And Song of Solomon 7:10 states, "I am my beloved's, and his desire is toward me." That connotes a good and loving relationship. So what is the woman's desire for her husband that came as a result of God's judgment in the garden of Eden? The answer comes when we define the word "desire."

From Strong's Concordance, we learn that in all three cases

"desire" is defined as a "sense of stretching out after; a longing," and its primary root meaning is "to run after or over." So although a wife has a longing desire for her husband and his love, God is saying it will now be coupled with a longing for and stretching forth for control!

Yes, the judgment placed on Eve is that she would now have an innate desire to take charge (to be in control) and her husband would have to "rule over" her. That is, he would need to resist her propensity to be boss in order to maintain his God-given authority as head of the house. "Rule" in this context means governing, not dictatorship. The sad fact is that you and I inherited from Eve the desire to be the boss—to be in control. "Your desire shall be for your husband, and he shall rule over you" (Genesis 3:16). Surely that doesn't describe you or me. Really? Well, yes. It describes you and me perfectly. We like being in charge.

The Lure of Being in Control

This universal truth is one of the most common reasons we fail to follow through on our good intentions in marriage. God designated our husbands as our head, but we want to be the head. It takes the help of the Holy Spirit for us to resist our natural propensity to take charge. Otherwise, we will try to control everything from the TV remote to when we visit our in-laws.

I've heard it said that when Eve covered herself with fig leaves, she became the first woman to wear the "plants" in the family! A role reversal where the wife leads and her husband follows violates one of the basic principles God ordained for marriage—the husband as head of his wife. Regardless of how it seems, a wife will never be head of her husband. I think the only way to accept this truth is to acknowledge that God is wiser than we are. It boils down to trusting God. After fifty years of marriage and many years of being bossy, I've never become the boss.

I remember one small class where a young woman bolted from

her chair upon hearing this truth. She said, "Oh no! That's what's wrong with my marriage. I tell my husband everything to do. I even told him what to wear this morning. Oh, I have to go call him right now."

Another young woman in class, who was divorced, delighted to hear this truth. She had just become engaged for the second time and said, "My fiancé nicknames me 'Miss Control.' I have been telling him I can't help being in control, that I was just born that way. And now I know it's true!"

Little had she realized that every woman since Eve has been "just born that way" and that we must be born again (receive Christ in our lives) in order to receive a life that is yielded to God and able to do His will. However, even with this new life born of the Spirit of God, we face the choice of living the old way or the new way. Our challenge is to make the right choice—to be willing to relinquish our cherished habit of being in control. But change doesn't happen all at once. It is progressive. That's encouraging.

The Wrong Tree: Leave It Alone

Eve, the mother of all living, was deceived. She ate forbidden fruit from the wrong tree. Can we not be in a similar vulnerable spot when we trust our own judgment above God's words or dismiss our husbands' words and give them little consideration? Regardless of how capable or accomplished we are, trusting only in ourselves can draw us (as well as our husbands) to the wrong tree and tempt us to taste attractive poison.

What is it you and I are facing that needs to be left alone (on the tree) because God say so? A man other than our own husband? God said we are not to taste adultery. What about the desire for a house as nice as our friend's house? God says we are not to covet our neighbor's house. And what do we need to leave on the tree because our husbands tell us to? That lovely antique buffet? A time-consuming commitment? A particular relationship? Just one more pair of shoes? Let's beware of what might bring poison into our marriages.

Sometimes an all-important activity needs to be left on the tree. We tend to forget it is our husbands who are all-important. I remember a young mother who took on the time-consuming volunteer job of chairing the lower school carnival. I understand the appeal of that because I once co-chaired a school carnival and loved every minute of it. But this particular mother was already over-committed, and taking on the additional commitment became burdensome. She said she was exhausted at the end of the day and had no energy left for her husband, her children, or even thinking about dinner.

Her husband told her that had she consulted him first, he would have advised her against taking it on, because her plate was already full. But the activity had such appeal that she made her decision independently of her husband. Instead, somewhere was a mother who had both the time and energy as well as the blessing of her husband.

The Wrong Voice

"Then to Adam He (God) said, 'Because you have heeded the voice of your wife, and have eaten from the tree of which I commanded you, saying, 'You shall not eat of it': Cursed is the ground for your sake; In toil you shall eat of it all the days of your life" (Genesis 3:17).

What dramatic words those are … "Because you have heeded the voice of your wife" … Instead of listening to what God told him, Adam listened to what Eve told him, and her words were contrary to God's words. The point is not that a husband should never listen to his wife. Genesis 21:12 proves otherwise. (In that scripture God tells Abraham to listen to his wife, Sarah.) The point is that like Eve, Adam followed a voice that contradicted God. So he fell into sin. God held Adam responsible because he was the head to whom the command had been given. Adam was not deceived.

The tragic result of Adam's sin was death—death in his spirit (alienated from God), in his soul (it became corrupt and rebellious), and eventually in his physical body. Then God sent Adam out of the garden to till the ground from which he was taken.

Do we see the problem? Given their freedom to choose, Adam and Eve asserted their independence and followed the wrong voice and ate from the wrong tree. They were wise in their own eyes, and it led to death. Our propensity to trust ourselves and reason things out is no less than theirs. God knows that, so He tells us to "Trust in the Lord with all your heart, and lean not on your own understanding. In all your ways acknowledge Him, and He shall direct your path" (Proverbs 3:5–6). That scripture is like an anchor to me, continually helping me live by faith in what God says rather than by what I think or feel.

Serpents on the Path

Eve was the first—but not the last— woman to face the cunning serpent. Enticing serpents will also appear on our paths to seduce us away from devotion to God and our husbands. Their voices are not the beautiful, pure words of God. They are the seemingly attractive words of the lying beast. As mentioned previously, they often come to our minds as questions such as, "Are you really meant to be a helper? Do you really need a head? Why should you yield to a husband who makes so many mistakes? Does your husband really deserve your respect?" We can be sure of this: God's ways are perfect.

The voice we follow depends upon whether we live naturally in the realm of our senses or supernaturally in the realm of faith in God and His words. Remarkably, many years later a serpent was placed on Jesus's path. Once again, the temptation involved food—this time offered to a very hungry man. But unlike Adam, Jesus resisted and overcame the devil by relying on God's words as He declared, "It is written...."

The result of each challenge and temptation we face in marriage depends upon whether we respond the way Adam and Eve did, or the way Jesus did. Adam and Eve succumbed to temptation because they put aside God's words and instead trusted their own judgment. On the other hand, Jesus was victorious over temptation because He depended completely upon His Father God and His trustworthy words. What a lesson for us!

At times I have thought, "Oh, if only Eve had sent the serpent to her husband instead of trying to handle him herself ... if only Eve had taken Adam's words seriously and not relied on her senses ... if only Eve had not eaten the fruit or offered it to Adam ... if only Eve had not acted so independently of God." But then I consider some of my own behavior, and I think, "If only I would learn from Eve's mistakes."

Summary

Adam and Eve vividly depict the frailty of every man and woman before his and her majestic Creator. God tells us, "He knows our frame; He remembers that we are dust" (Psalm 103:14). Yet we tend to think we are mighty and wise. We outgrow the trusting child who sings, "Jesus loves me this I know," and ends with the words, "Little ones to Him belong. They are weak, but He is strong."

This first marriage uncovers the root of every problem in marriage. That root is sin, and it is characterized by our selfish and proud desire for independence—not only from God, but from our husbands.

This sin is manifested in marriage through our rebellion against the authority placed over us (resisting both God and our husbands); our propensity to trust in our own wisdom and lead our husbands; our husbands' irresponsibility and abdication of leadership; our failure to respect our husbands and their words; and above all, our failure to completely trust the goodness and faithfulness of almighty God and His Word. Each of these hindrances to marital intimacy is addressed in the following chapters. Here is the good news in advance: God offers us the remedy for each one.

Even in a perfect world with a perfect spouse, Adam and Eve acted without regard to God and His words. They violated every principle addressed in this book. The helper didn't help. The head didn't lead. The head didn't follow his Head. The wife listened to a strange serpent rather than her husband. Reverence for God, respect for the husband, and protection of the wife were missing.

May the disaster that resulted be the blinking yellow light that warns us of our need to lay down our independence and live by what God is telling us—by every word He speaks. Even amid all of our failings, God continues to love us and help us move beyond good intentions and genuinely love and cherish our husbands the way we promised.

> *Do not be wise in your own eyes; Fear*
> *the Lord and depart from evil.*
> *—Proverbs 3:7*

Dear Lord, Thank You for showing me what I am like apart from You. I confess that I often cherish my independence and tend to take charge of everything, depriving my husband of the right to lead me. Please begin to repair any damage I have already done by my independent and controlling ways.

Also please give me a heart that is willing to hear and heed Your words. Meanwhile, please give my husband the desire and wisdom to lovingly lead our family. Thank You. Amen.

Is He Really My Head?

For the husband is head of the wife, as also
Christ is head of the church ...
—Ephesians 5:23

But I want you to know that the head of every man is Christ,
the head of woman is man, and the head of Christ is God.
—1 Corinthians 11:3

I was visiting a store to buy three-by-five cards and small stickers to place on each card. As I handed the merchandise to the lady behind the counter, she smiled at the cute little bear stickers and asked what I was going to do with them. I told her I was using them to place on cards with the scripture, "The husband is head of the wife." Well, she threw back her head in almost hysterical laughter and replied, "I can't believe you really said that." There was a second of silence, and then by the grace of God, I very gently said, "I didn't say that. God did." At that, she looked at me rather harshly and said nothing.

I understand that dear lady. She knows men and women are equally valuable. But what she doesn't know or accept is that even though God created men and women with equal value, He gave husbands and wives different roles in marriage. He's the head; she's the helper. These roles are God's idea and His decision. They are fixed forever in each and every generation. "Forever, O Lord, Your word is settled in heaven" (Psalm 119:89). That consistency of His words is a gift to us. Otherwise we have no absolute truths to which we can cling.

Indeed, God has ordained an order of authority for all of creation. It is the way He governs. "I want you to know that the head of every man is Christ, the head of woman is man, and the head of Christ is God" (1Corinthians 11:3). And as mentioned previously, children are to obey their parents "in the Lord." God-given authority is not punishment. It's a gift that prevents chaos.

Although there is much I don't know about this tough subject, I am sharing my limited understanding. It is what helps me accept and even be thankful for my husband as my head—most of the time.

Key Characteristics of Headship

So what is headship? Two specific characteristics lie at the heart of biblical headship. According to Vine's Expository Dictionary, the word "head" in the Ephesians passage written previously refers to two things: authority and direction. Just as the church recognizes the authority of Jesus and His words that lead us, so the wife is meant to acknowledge the authority that God has given to her husband and his words to lead the family.

In a word, the husband bears the ultimate responsibility for the decisions and direction of the family. As his helper, the wife is responsible for being the other part of the decision-making process. Her input is as valuable as his. Headship does not mean that the husband is wiser or that he makes all the decisions while the wife quietly stands by. Nor does it mean he and his wife cannot defer to each other or compromise. It means whereas a husband and wife share their thoughts and desires with the hope of coming to mutual decisions, the husband has been given the authority to make final decisions. It is the husband whom God holds accountable for the decisions and direction of the family. We see this first in the marriage of Adam and Eve.

Adam was the one to whom God gave direction not to eat from one specific tree. So even though Eve took the first bite, it was Adam whom God held responsible. The buck stopped with the husband.

I used to work for an oil company. In my department, I knew who carried the responsibility for decisions. It wasn't I. But I never felt unimportant. My job was valuable, and my boss depended upon me to help him in a variety of ways. After all, we were shareholders in the same company, and we wanted the company to prosper. So also in a marriage, the head and the helper, equal in value but different in their roles, are appointed by God to work together in ways that benefit the family.

Can we not trust God for the way He designed marriage? He even designed the parts of our bodies to have diverse functions. Each part is unique and valuable. And each part has its own job to do. He who made eyes that see, arms that hug, and taste buds that celebrate chocolate, is He not the same one who designed the husband and wife to have different functions? Can a husband carry a baby in the womb? The differing roles and functions of husbands and wives stem from the heart and wisdom of God.

FROM PERFECT JESUS TO IMPERFECT HUSBAND

The Same Response: Listen!

Since the Lord tells us the husband is head of the wife as also Christ is head of the church, let's consider how we apply that to our marriages. What is it about the way we are to respond to Jesus as the perfect head of the church that we can translate to how we respond to our husbands as our imperfect head? For me, that is the big question.

The first consideration that makes sense to me is to ask myself how Jesus as our spiritual head leads us. Jesus leads us primarily by His Word and by His Spirit. By His words in the Bible, He speaks to us. And by the Holy Spirit, we hear Him and are given the grace to step out in faith and do what He says. Authority and direction! His words have authority, and He directs us through them. Jesus said, "My sheep hear My voice ... and they follow Me" (John 10:27).

Therefore, based on my belief that we (the church) follow our head, Jesus, primarily by listening to His words, I likewise aim to honor my husband's headship by really listening to what he says. That includes looking to him for advice, opinions, ideas, and direction. In other words, I am acknowledging the importance of his thoughts and words. I hold onto his advice. Lest we forget, Adam's words to Eve disappeared like mist when the serpent came along and beguiled her with *his* words.

A second way I aim to honor my husband's headship is by acknowledging his authority to make final decisions regarding the family when necessary. Frankly, on a day-to-day basis, responding to my husband as my head is not something I consciously think about. Many, if not most, of our decisions and direction each day can be made independently of each other.

It is when we disagree on major issues (e.g., job, home, health, money, or family) that we are confronted with the fact that someone needs to be designated as the final decision-maker after all else has failed. The Lord wants us to know that He has given that authority and responsibility to our husbands. They have the final say on family decisions. That is the wisdom of God. It can be freeing to accept that truth.

From my observation, one problem we share as wives is our failure to value our husband's words (just as our husbands might fail to value the words of their head, Jesus, or of us as their wives). We might not realize how often we listen half-heartedly or with a dismissive attitude—or maybe not listen at all. What we can do instead is to begin cultivating a sensitivity to the presence of God because He enables us to really hear what our husbands are saying. Otherwise we might keep on talking until we have the last word. I wonder how many times I haven't been quiet long enough to know what my husband's last word might be.

Indeed our husbands' headship gives them the authority to have the last word on a matter. That is their prerogative—to make the final call when necessary. But since marriage is meant to be two working together as one, there should be give-and-take on both sides. Think in terms of the word "collaboration." To collaborate is to work one with another, to cooperate willingly. It is not a case of the husband ruling and making all the decisions.

In fact, as part of loving his wife, a husband might often defer to her and her desires. When a marriage relationship is right, love and consideration for each other are part of collaborating and discussing the issues. Nevertheless, God holds our husbands accountable for final decisions and direction, and we need to be willing to accept those decisions with grace and not anger. Regarding direction, unless a wife is called to follow illegal or immoral direction from her husband, she does well to follow his lead.

What Does Your Husband Say?

So what does your husband say? What does my husband say? How much voice do we give them in our social life, our vacations, or which relatives to visit? And what do our husbands say about the choice of schools, churches, and neighborhoods? Do we tend to make decisions that impact our family independently of our husbands? What do our husbands say about how our money and/or time together is spent, how our homes are decorated, or how our children are disciplined, including what they watch on TV? Do we accept invitations without knowing if our husbands want to accept?

I have a friend who didn't consult her husband and his calendar before sending out party invitations. With embarrassment she had to retract all of them after learning her husband wasn't available that weekend. She was struck with the realization she had given no thought to her husband when making her plans.

That might sound like an unlikely situation, but I've learned it is not. I recall the time an acquaintance told her friends she was absolutely frantic about choosing the right school for her child. She stayed awake at night, vacillating between choosing one school over the other. When one of her friends asked what her husband thought, she said, "I don't know. I've never asked." She then took her friend's advice and asked her husband for his input. He had a definite and reasonable opinion, and the frantic wife was no longer frantic.

I could relate countless stories where wives simply neglected to consult their husbands before making important decisions. A memorable example is the time a friend asked me to join her during a church service as she went to the altar for prayer. She was the picture of physical beauty—smiling, radiant, and altogether lovely. She looked into the eyes of the pastor and said, "Will you please pray for me? I don't know whether or not to quit my job."

The pastor looked into her beaming face and asked, "Are you married?" After she replied "yes," the pastor had one more question. He asked, "What does your husband say?"

I can still see the countenance on my friend's face. It fell. Her joy vanished. That was not the answer she was looking for. Oh, what a wise pastor! He was responding to a wife who had left her husband out of the equation. Lest we forget, God has provided our husbands to help us with direction and decisions when we need them. But do we accept His provision or neglect or reject it?

Not only is it important for us to hear what our husbands have to say about a matter, but our children need to hear and respect what their dad says. Even though both parents have authority over their children, a wife's desire to control can eclipse her husband's voice. Sadly, some children never know the beauty and importance of their father's headship. Insofar as it depends upon you and me, let us bless our children by walking in harmony under the leadership of their father … even the father we think is not as wise as we are. That's an opportunity to live by faith while we pray and wait for our husbands to receive God's wisdom and direction.

When parents don't walk as one, a child has no place to go for definitive guidelines. Matthew 12:25 tells us that "every house divided against itself will not stand." Children are perceptive, and where there is division, they learn to approach the parent who will give the answer they want.

We do well to consider our tendency to make major decisions regarding our children independently of our husbands. Even with minor decisions, there are times when a loving response to our children might be, "I'll ask your dad" or "We'll wait and see what Daddy says." Children learn respect for authority from their parents, so let's remember the question, "What does your husband say?"

Church Attendance: A Sticky Issue

What about church attendance? Where do we go when there is disagreement? Once our husbands know our desire and preference in churches, it is good to leave it in the Lord's hands. We can ask God to intervene and have His way with us. Only He can change hearts and minds. It might even be ours that needs changing. Meanwhile we do well to follow our husbands and sit beside them at whatever Christian church they, as head of the family, choose to attend. Frankly, there are plenty of women who would be thrilled to sit with your husband or mine in church or anywhere. Let's be sure it is we who sit with them.

Are we any less likely to be deceived into disobedience than Eve was? We are adept at rationalizing our position. When we are eager for our husbands to become responsible spiritual leaders, our natural instinct is to try leading them to the church we believe is most beneficial. But what is most beneficial? Obedience. God is not dependent upon us to shake up our husbands spiritually. We need to ask ourselves which is more important: being in a specific church each Sunday or being obedient to God.

Catholic or Protestant?

A potential area of grief is experienced when one spouse is Catholic and the other is Protestant. If that is our case, we can let obedience swallow our grief. We simply follow our husbands to church. If we are Catholics, we can attend mass at some time other than during the time we sit with our husbands on Sunday mornings. If we are Protestants, we can enjoy Bible studies during the week and then sit at our husband's side during the Catholic service. We are not hindered in our spiritual growth by where we spend that hour or so on Sunday. We are hindered in our spiritual growth when we disobey. Not following our head is disobedience.

One night at dinner, I noticed a Roman Catholic priest seated at a nearby table. I asked him how he dealt with the problem of church attendance in a Catholic/Protestant marriage. In a voice filled with conviction, he said the husband has to be confirmed as spiritual head of the home. Unless he takes the leadership, the priest said the home will suffer. In a word, he tells his women parishioners they do not have to give up their Catholicism, but they do have to go to church where their husbands lead.

Indeed, the issue of church attendance, like much else in marriage, can be resolved with the simple but important question, "What does your husband say?"

Difficult Situations

My personal belief is that next to the word of God, a husband's words, unless they are riddled with lies or hostility, are probably more valuable than we ever dream they are. The fact is, the words we follow reveal who has authority in our eyes. And yet there might be areas where following a husband's lead is really difficult.

I remember a woman telling me she seriously questioned following her husband's request. He wanted her to quit her job and stay home with their children. But she didn't want to quit. Furthermore she said she believed God wanted her to continue working. She said she knew she should follow God rather than her husband. That was a touchy situation because whereas we are to seek the Lord for personal direction, we are also to look to our husbands for advice.

Consider this: God does not send mixed signals. If following what we think the Lord is telling us means defying our husbands, we need to question whether we are truly hearing from God. We can be deceived into thinking we are hearing from God when we are not, especially if we think He is telling us something we want to hear anyway.

What we can do in a questionable situation is communicate to the Lord that we want to honor His word that says the husband is the head. But meanwhile we ask Him to intervene and change our husband's heart and mind (or ours) if He wants to lead us in a different direction. The exception to this would be situations where we believe following our husbands would lead us to sin. In that case, we must refuse to follow. An example frequently used is that of a husband wanting his wife to sign a dishonest IRS tax return. That is a situation where a wife should legitimately refuse to follow.

It is a challenge to follow our husbands when we disagree with their judgment. But we can be comforted by something God tells us. He is looking at our hearts, and He knows those who want to do the right thing (1 Samuel 16:7). Therefore, as a general rule, I believe that unless our husbands lead us into sin or a sinful situation, we do well to listen to them and follow their lead. God honors those who honor Him with their trusting obedience.

Practical Challenge

A few years ago I faced what might seem like a minor challenge to follow my husband. But was it really minor? My husband is disciplined and exercises regularly. You can guess the rest. He requested several times that I, too, begin to exercise on a regular basis. Even though I knew it would be valuable and energizing, exercise bored me. So I became adept at finding ways to avoid it. At some point though, I realized God might be speaking to me through my husband. I remembered that after my mother was diagnosed with Parkinson's disease, her physician (as well as my dad) encouraged her to exercise, but she also found excuses not to.

So wanting to stay in good health and believing the Lord and my husband had my best interest at heart, I made a decision. I would exercise in spite of my feelings. That was not an easy decision. But what motivated me was a certain fear of the Lord. I knew then—and I know now—that the two relationships (the one with the Lord and the one with my husband) are connected. I also wanted to stay healthy. So I exercised.

But there is a postscript to this story. My exercise program was short-lived. After about a year I drifted back to my old habit. I stopped exercising. Oh, how easy it is to return to old habits, even with the best of intentions. And now, several years later, my internist tells me that I must exercise in order to combat osteoporosis. If only I had listened.

Is there something your husband has been suggesting, asking, or telling you to do? Take care not to dismiss or ignore his words. God hears every word our husbands say to us. Perhaps He even prompts them to say some of those words.

The example of exercising might seem insignificant, but is it? Who has weighed the words of a husband except God? The words Adam spoke to Eve about not eating from one particular tree, were they "mere" words? Apparently Eve thought so. After all, it was surely just a trivial thing to eat that pretty piece of fruit.

It is sobering to realize one way God has chosen to lead us is through our husbands. Consider this amazing example from Matthew 2:13: After Mary had given birth to Jesus, an angel of the Lord appeared to her husband Joseph in a dream, saying, "Arise, take the young Child and His mother, flee to Egypt, and stay there until I bring you word …" Again, in two later verses, God spoke to Joseph, the husband of Mary, to lead her and the child.

You and I might have expected God to address Mary rather than Joseph because she was the favored vessel who bore His Son. Furthermore, because Jesus was conceived by the Holy Spirit, Joseph was not the biological father (Matthew 1:18). Yet in His infinite wisdom, God spoke through the husband to lead his family.

Summary

Consider this: Many people don't acknowledge Jesus Christ as the Son of God or as the head of the church. But that doesn't change the fact that He is. The issue for them is that their failure to acknowledge the truth eternally affects their lives and destiny. So it is in marriage. God has appointed the husband to be the head of his wife. Our failure to acknowledge that truth will not change the fact. But it will affect how we treat our husbands and thus will impact the quality and future of our marriages.

And consider this: Jesus has a head (1 Corinthians 11:3). Consider how Jesus listened to His head—the Father—and worked with and not against Him. In fact, together Father, Son, and Holy Spirit created the heavens and earth. Together they created man. Together they redeemed man. All three persons are involved in different ways to bring about the salvation of man. And although they are equally God, their roles differ.

Jesus Christ came as our Savior. That is His role. And even though He is equal to God the Father, He did not grasp at that equality. Instead He humbled Himself before His Father and obeyed Him right up to death. As a result, His Father exalted Him (Philippians 2:5–9).

The Lord wants us to have that same attitude—one that yields, not grasps. In other words, even though we and our husbands have equal value, the role of headship belongs to them, not us. It is not ours to reach out for. Nothing good comes from trying to grab something that doesn't belong to us.

Can you imagine resentment or competition among the Father, Son, and Holy Spirit because they have different roles? Can you imagine Jesus telling His Father that He doesn't like His role as Savior, so He decided not to go to the cross? That sounds outrageous, and yet have we ever thought to ourselves, "I don't like my role as helper or my husband's role as head. I'm equal to my husband, so I don't need to listen to him"?

And consider this: God made man first. He charged the man with tending and keeping the garden. He commanded the man not to eat from the Tree of the Knowledge of Good and Evil. He gave the man authority to name the animals. He made the woman from the man and for the man and brought her to the man. He gave the man authority to name the woman. And yet a man's authority as head of his wife does not negate the fact that man and woman were created equal in worth and value and were both given dominion over the earth. Furthermore man and woman share equally in God's inheritance of grace.

And last of all, consider this: God formed man to lead his wife. Not only is the male body generally stronger than the female body, but God created the male body to take the lead in the most intimate of all moments. For how can sexual union occur without the male being ready? And who proposes marriage? Truly the husband initiates and invites; the wife responds. It is a beautiful reflection of the kingdom of God where the Bridegroom Jesus calls, and the bride (the church) responds—where the Bridegroom leads and the bride follows.

Let's trust the beauty of God's ways. Headship on earth is a reflection of headship in heaven. It is the way the Lord has chosen to govern.

Even though there are times you and I might fight it, I know deep down inside that I need a head. And I know my husband needs a head. And both of us have been given one. Let's thank God that we have an ultimate head named Jesus who is sovereign and in control. He loves us beyond our comprehension. And our husbands' headship is one of His gifts to us.

As for God, His way is perfect; The word of the Lord is proven …
—Psalm 18:30

Dear Lord, I have not been a very good listener, and I often fail to give much weight to my husband's words. I simply haven't acknowledged him as my head. So for the many times and ways I have ignored the authority You have given him as my head, please forgive me.

When I need it, please remind me of the question, "What does my husband say?" I want to encourage his leadership, not hinder him. So please help me look to him for advice and direction when I need it. Also help me value his words and opinions as I stand behind his decisions. When I believe his decisions are unwise, please give me the grace to be kind and to trust You with the results.

Just as I am learning to listen more to my husband, I really need my husband to listen more to me and to value what I think and say. Please help! Thank You, dear Lord. Amen.

Having a Head without a Headache

The word of the Lord is proven; He is a
shield to all who trust in Him.
—Psalm 18:30

Staying healthy is better than having to get healed. And accepting God's word that a husband is his wife's head is better than having to take aspirin to deal with it.

There is a beautiful picture painted in the Bible that has kept me out of the aspirin bottle. It is a picture of being covered—protected— secure. The principle is that our husbands' headship is a gift from God that provides an invisible protective covering for us.

Think about a Covering

There is something intrinsically comforting to me about being covered, especially in bed at night. From the beginning of time, one way God provided for His people was in the form of a covering. After Adam and Eve sinned and recognized their nakedness, God covered them with the skin of a sacrificed animal. That covering was God's provision, pointing to the sacrificial system whereby Jesus, the Lamb of God, would sacrifice His life on the cross to provide forgiveness of our sins.

Years later during Passover, when the Israelites did as God instructed and placed blood on the doorposts and lintels of their houses, that covering was God's gift to spare them and protect them from His deadly judgment on the Egyptians (Exodus 12). And later when God led His people out of Egypt, He provided a cloud covering by day and a pillar of fire by night. (What a night-light!)

These coverings were given for the stated purpose, "to lead the way" (Exodus 13:21; Numbers 9:15–17). Even today as God leads His children by the Holy Spirit, they are covered with invisible garments of salvation and robes of righteousness (Isaiah 61:10).

I submit that just as Jesus provides Himself to His bride (the church) as her spiritual covering of protection and guidance, similarly He provides our husbands for us and our families. We are under the covering of their authority as our God-given protectors who are created to "lead the way."

This doesn't sit well with our natural desire for control. Furthermore, we might doubt our husband's ability to lead us. So it is natural to dismiss them and what they say. It's hard to accept the concept of headship unless we recognize there is a spiritual dimension to marriage. Our marriages are meant to reflect the relationship between Jesus and His church. The implication is that just as Jesus was given to the church as her head, so are our husbands given to us as our head. Both signify staying under that authority as if it were a covering.

One of the most beautiful images of God as a protective covering over His people is from Psalm 91:4: "He shall cover you with His feathers, and under His wings you shall take refuge." What peace that gives us. What safety. What security. Covered.

Uncovered: My Mistake

Years ago when I was a young Christian, I befriended a woman whom I thought was "spiritual." Several times my husband expressed concern that this woman was strange. I acknowledged that she was different, but I continued to see her and think of her as a friend. I was wrong. She was an adversary who envied my good marriage and me.

At some point, I began to be uncomfortable around this woman. She was giving me unsolicited "spiritual" advice that just didn't sound right. And her negativity left me uneasy. I finally realized she really was strange, and I ended the relationship. Sometime later I learned from a friend that this strange woman said she wanted nothing good to come my way. On the contrary!

In hindsight, I see that had I thought about my husband as my God-given head, or covering, I would have taken his concern and opinion seriously. Hopefully I would have either backed off or broken off from the so-called friendship. God had given me a husband as a covering, but I failed to recognize it and act upon it. I became a sad example of trusting my own judgment. Clearly God gave discernment to my husband. It was discernment I did not have.

By trusting myself and not giving weight to my husband's words, it was as if I had gotten out from under my human covering and into a place of spiritual vulnerability. That is, I was more vulnerable to deception. That was Eve's undoing. She dismissed Adam's words and succumbed to the enticing words of the wily devil. Seeing this in hindsight makes me more grateful than ever that God, through His goodness and mercy, set me free from the woman's grip.

I am reminded of a woman who, like me, also learned the lesson of listening seriously to her husband's words. In this case, her husband told her that he no longer wanted their young daughter to play with a particular child. His reason was that he distrusted the child's father. That devastated this woman. She couldn't imagine how to break off the children's play dates. Nevertheless, with reluctance, she decided to listen to her husband.

For a certain period of time she gave excuses to her friend as to why the children could not get together. But one day the mother experienced a moment of weakness. She reasoned that it was probably all right for her daughter to go to her friend's house to play. After all, her daughter was begging her to go. And after all, the two little girls were such good friends. And after all, they hadn't been together for quite a while. So she allowed it.

Later in the day, she learned that when her daughter arrived at the friend's house to play, the mother was not home. Only the father was there. The woman was devasted because she realized she had unwittingly left her daughter to spend the morning not only with her playmate, but with the very man her husband didn't trust. By the grace of God, all went well.

The fact is, neither this woman nor I was thinking in terms of coverings, or headship, or authority when we failed to consider our husband's warnings. We were just doing what comes naturally, trusting our own judgment.

Could there be an area today where you and I might be underestimating or even ignoring our husband's suggestion or advice? If so, may God mercifully convict us and change our habit of not giving serious thought to what our husbands say.

As a postscript, among many beautiful examples throughout scripture of the blessedness of being covered is a verse in the story of Ruth. When Ruth approached Boaz, the kinsman-redeemer who was to become her husband, she laid down beside his feet and said to him, "I am Ruth your maid. So spread your covering over your maid, for you are a close relative" (Ruth 3:9 NAS). In the NKJV, Ruth says, "Take your maidservant under your wing, for you are a close relative." In effect, she is saying, "Marry me! Be my covering."

Think about an Umbrella

An often-used illustration of a husband being his wife's covering is the picture of an umbrella. Just as an umbrella is needed to cover and protect us from some of life's rainy or stormy days, so do we need our husband's invisible covering of protection and leadership.

What if our husbands are not the kind of umbrella we expected or wanted? Perhaps they don't love us as they should. Maybe they are irresponsible, lazy, distant. Does that make our umbrella useless?

No. God knows the makeup of our husbands, and He still calls them our head. He knows exactly how to equip them to be responsible, protective, wise leaders. So we pray for that, even as we thank God for providing a covering we cannot see.

It isn't natural to think of headship as a gift from God. But Ephesians 1:22 says God *gave* Jesus to be head over the church, His bride, just as He *gave* the husband to be head over his wife. Both are gifts to be received. But thinking that way is foreign to our natural minds. It takes the ever-present Holy Spirit to help us renew our minds to think like God does. How we think makes all the difference in how we treat our husbands. Let's ask Him to help us see headship as a gift.

Think about Being a "Neck"

I heard a wise teacher suggest that a wife should think of herself as a "neck"—the support system that upholds her husband as her "head." What a vivid picture! And what a necessary part of the body the neck is! If your husband or mine seems to be a droopy head— that is, one who is dejected or fails to lead—then let's consider the condition of his neck. Are we doing enough to support and encourage our husbands? Or are we complaining and perhaps putting pressure on them for more? It could be a new house or car, a club membership, an expensive trip, or whatever puts pressure on our husbands for "more" and says, "I am not content." Droopy heads are not good.

Let's value being the "neck" that can support and encourage our husbands like no one else can. Meanwhile, the same teacher stated that a wise neck has the ability and privilege to turn the head—to influence her husband. And that is as it should be.

Godly leading is a tremendous responsibility. Our support is invaluable. Part of our role as helpers is sharing our insights and opinions in the decision-making process. But our suggestions and input are not directives. Our natural tendency is to be insistent, even pushy, about our opinions, especially when we are convinced we are right. So after years of trying to direct rather than suggest, I have learned a soft and more gracious way to participate in decision-making. It is simply to say, "Do you think we should consider ...?" That way, my idea is placed before my husband without his ideas or authority being challenged by an insistent, always-right wife.

Speaking of head and neck, consider that in both the physical realm and the spiritual realm, there is a head joined to a body, and they function as one. Where the head leads, the body follows. Even in a natural birth, the head usually comes first; the body follows.

In the spiritual realm, when we acknowledge Jesus as our spiritual head, we (the church) are called the body of Christ, and we follow Him by listening and doing what He says. Head and body are not independent of each other. They are designed to work together.

Think about Staying Connected

If our marriages lack "oneness" or unity, it's time to evaluate our tendency to disconnect from our head like Eve did. I have actually seen a headless creature. It was our cat's prized, newly captured chameleon that got crunched in two. He proudly dropped it right in front of me, leaving a revolting sight, because the tail end of the body was detached from the head, and it continued to flutter about for a period of time. A body disconnected from its head is seriously ugly.

Yet it is not uncommon for us to unintentionally detach ourselves from our husbands. When I hear women discuss their marriage woes, there is usually a sprinkling of words like, "I think," "I feel," or "I want," which are then followed by "but he ..."

When we get around to the subject of a woman's desire to be in control, I've never known a woman (including myself) who hasn't admitted that she is often such a woman. We might even become obnoxious when we don't get our way. Perhaps we are convinced we have better judgment than our husbands, and we are frustrated at their lack of wisdom. It can involve anything from spending money to raising children. We might genuinely believe we would make a better head.

That is when we need to acknowledge that God's ways are perfect. He can be trusted with our husband's headship. If we try to reason this out in our own understanding, we will be in Eve's shoes. Remember, she rationalized and figured out all the ways it was all right to eat that fruit. But she was all wrong. I've worn Eve's shoes. And the longer I've worn them, the more uncomfortable they've become.

After many years of marriage, I can say with conviction that it is good to have a head. Ever since I realized I was not given the responsibility for the final decisions and direction of our family, I was relieved (freed) of a burden I was not meant to bear. And I have a happier husband. Furthermore, my shoes are comfortable. Usually.

Let's consider being connected as a strong neck to our husbands as our head. Our husbands need all the support they can get from us.

Think about Entrusting Him to His Head

One of the best ways to avoid letting our husband's headship give us a headache is to remember that our husbands have a head—a perfect head (1 Corinthians 11:3). Even better news is that His name is Jesus, not "wife." We are not responsible for our husbands. God initiated their headship and assumes full responsibility for it.

Our job is to entrust our husbands completely into God's hands through prayer and to do our part to obey what the Lord says to us. Trust and obey. That's not easy because even if we do our part, we might think our husbands have a long way to go before they do their part. This results in our habit of helping God bring about all the marvelous changes we have in mind for our husbands.

The first delicious role we tackle is the role of "teacher"—the one who helps her husband learn how to behave. The second role is "convictor—the one who brings to her husband's attention all of his shortfalls. Akin to these roles are "judge" and "mother." Are you and I never quite through "telling" our husbands? And how easy and natural it is to make sure we have that last word!

The fact is, God gave the job of teaching and convicting our husbands to someone else— the Holy Spirit. "But the Helper, the Holy Spirit … *He will teach* you all things …" (John 14:26). "And when He (the Holy Spirit) has come, *He will convict* the world of sin, and of righteousness and of judgment" (John 16:8, emphasis mine).

There is one major source of help if we want to see changes in our husbands. That source is the person of the Holy Spirit, the Helper. Only He can change us. We don't have to hound our husbands with our complaints! Nor do we have to tell our friends about our husband's faults. Our job is to pray and wait in faith while we do our part. Therein lies our hope. What is our part? To treat them like the head God says they are. We can begin by paying more attention to them and respectfully listening to what they are saying.

Think about a Possible Role Reversal

From the time Eve took that first bite of forbidden fruit and gave some to Adam, human nature has not changed. We want our independence to do things our way. In fact, we want to be the head. And husbands want their independence to do things their way without looking to the Lord to lead them. So it is natural for husbands to renege on their role as responsible leaders. And it is natural for us to try to fill that void in leadership. Their failure to lead feeds right into our waiting hands. We are ready to take charge! Away we go! And away go our husbands, following behind. Each weakness feeds off the other. A vicious cycle begins. We lead; they follow. Thus comes the toxic ingredient in many marriages: a role reversal.

When our Bible study was small, I posed a question to eighteen women in the class, asking, "If your husband were in a men's Bible study on marriage, what would you like for him to be taught?" The number-one response was "spiritual leadership." A close second was "learning how to love me." The failure of a husband to assume his role as a responsible and loving head is not uncommon.

I remember one of our young sons laughing at the subject of headship. He said, "Mom, you know Mrs. Anderson (not real name) runs the whole show in that family. How can you possibly say Mr. Anderson is the head of Mrs. Anderson?" I explained that as aggressive as she was in ruling the family, Mrs. Anderson was not and never will be the head. Her husband had simply reneged on his role, and she was trying to fill it.

In contrast to husbands who abdicate their responsibility to lead are the husbands who misunderstand their role and "overreact" to their headship, abusing it in various ways. They might be demanding men who reduce their wives to lonely women who are given no voice in decisions or are treated without respect. For wives who feel trapped by demanding husbands who try to rule their lives, counsel is well advised.

Think about Getting Out of the Way

Could it be that our husbands are willing to lead us but are unsuccessful because we stand in the way, clinging to our zeal for control? Perhaps our husbands are trying to lead us and we don't see it. Or could it be our husbands have heard us criticize them so often that we are the reason they are passive or indifferent?

When husbands say indifferently, "Do whatever you want," could it be they have heard us override their suggestions or decisions often enough that they know their opinions have little value in our eyes? So perhaps they figure, "Why bother trying to lead?"

What about the husbands who simply clam up and tune us out? Could it be they have frequently been put down or had their judgment challenged? A defensive, stubborn, or angry husband might be the result of having been continually criticized. If we would listen to ourselves, would we hear critical words that condemn or gracious words that encourage and give life?

One friend said when she asked her husband why he didn't tell her his opinion sooner, he replied, "Have you ever tried to argue with you?" Our husbands need to know we are on their side in life even when we disagree with them. Getting our way is not a worthy goal. Becoming one with our husbands is. So when they suggest something we think is unreasonable, rather than blurting out the negative words that are waiting to erupt, perhaps we can at least say, "I'll think about it."

We rarely see ourselves at fault or contributing to a bad situation. A friend told me she attended a bridal shower where the bride-to-be was gifted with a mirror. Attached was a tag that read, "To look into when you want to see the other half of the problem!"

Think about Responding with Grace

With or without our help, our husbands will likely make numerous decisions and judgment calls with which we disagree. That's the time for us to lean on the Holy Spirit to respond to those unwelcome decisions with grace. Actually our responses could be more important than the decisions because they are like blocks that either build up or tear down our relationship. Who will better fulfill the role of a godly head, the one who is supported and encouraged or the one who is criticized with an "I told you so"?

I know a man who has a weakness for expensive cars. He once had his eye on a car that his wife knew they could not comfortably afford. She told him why she thought he should defer the purchase. He bought it anyway. Sometime later the payments became burdensome, and he had to let the car go.

His wise wife chose not to say, "I told you so." She patiently loved him through it and trusted God to use the incident to teach her husband what he needed to learn in the area of financial responsibility. That was doing what comes supernaturally—showing grace or undeserved favor—which emanated from the Spirit of God. Imagine the difference in their relationship had she responded naturally with condemning words. It makes such a difference when we let the Holy Spirit lead us and control our restless tongue. He gives us the grace to respond in a way that helps develop and sustain a good relationship.

As we pray for our husbands to assume the role of leader or make decisions more often, let's listen to ourselves. Does our tone of voice encourage them to lead us in a loving way?

And Finally, Think About a Crown

Proverbs 12:4 says, "An excellent wife is the crown of her husband..." Where does a crown belong? Clearly on the head. A friend who grasped the beauty of this scripture wrote, "It occurred to me that in order to be his crown, I have to make him my head. And I thought, what an incredible privilege it is to be a crown ... I never want my husband to be without his crown." That crown, you see, is symbolic of the love, honor, and respect she has bestowed upon him as her head and her king. Imagine—he wears a crown because his wife treats him like a king. How beautiful! May you and I take pleasure in envisioning our husbands wearing their crowns.

Summary

The principle of governing through headship was God's idea. It reaches from heaven to earth—from the Father to the Son to the husband to the wife to the children. When we accept Jesus Christ as our spiritual head, it brings a responsibility to accept our husbands as our earthly head. It is that simple. But it is not that easy.

What comes easily and naturally is our sense of autonomy. We think we can get along fine without acknowledging our husbands as our head. So we go our own way and watch the relationship we hoped for begin to elude us. Can we have a close relationship with our husbands when we rebuff their authority and dismiss their importance in our lives?

I remember a wedding reception where the new bride walked throughout the reception with her hands on her hips. At one point she approached the bandleader with one hand still on her hip and a finger from the other hand pointing at his face. I was stunned.

Sitting beside me was a friend who also recognized the implications of the bride's demeanor. She whispered, "I wonder how long this marriage will last."

Before the reception was over, the bride surprised the groom and guests by announcing that she would be retaining her maiden name. The marriage lasted a very short time.

We can have a head without a headache, but it is only when we take God's word seriously. It is a hard truth, but our husbands— without having earned or deserved it and even perhaps behaving like it—have been appointed by God to be head of their wives. That means God holds them responsible for the final direction and decisions in the marriage. So let's cooperate with them by giving our input and then by listening to them attentively as we consider their words more seriously than ever. God's gracious Holy Spirit is here to help us.

Perhaps this wonderful African proverb, given to me by a friend, sums it up: "The hen sees the sun rise but leaves it to the rooster to announce it."

> O *Lord my God, You are very great: You are clothed with honor and majesty, Who cover Yourself with light as with a garment, Who stretch out the heavens like a curtain.*
> —*Psalm 104:1–2*

> *Now therefore, listen to Me, my children, For blessed are those who keep my ways.*
> —*Proverbs 8:32*

Dear Lord, please help me get my arms around this teaching. I know I need eyes of faith to see my husband as my earthly head. I can list a lot of reasons why it seems he is not my head, but I realize that would be contradicting You. So by Your grace, please help me appreciate my husband as my head as I seek his advice and pay more attention to what he says.

Please also help me give up my zeal for independence and control so I don't hinder or decimate my husband's potential as a responsible leader. And then please mold him into a wise husband who appreciates me and treats me with love. Thank You. Amen.

Flesh or Spirit?

It is the Spirit who gives life; the flesh profits nothing.
The words that I speak to you are spirit, and they are life.
—John 6:63

Years ago, a college professor drilled three words into my ears that I will never forget. Repeatedly, week by week, he would say, "Behavior is caused."

Yes, behavior has a cause. There is a reason we behave the way we do. And much of our behavior is a function of whether we are walking in the flesh or walking in the Spirit. By that, I mean whether we are allowing our old self-centered nature with which we were born to direct our lives or whether we are allowing the new nature born of God to direct our behavior.

This subject is especially interesting to me because when I learned the difference between flesh and Spirit, I began to understand "me," and my behavior was positively affected, especially as a wife. I realized there were two distinct choices before me in how I might respond to any given situation.

A Problem: Flesh

When you and I think of the word "inheritance," we likely think of something good that is passed on from generation to generation. But in every generation since Adam, something not good is passed on. What's not good is the human nature that is corrupted by sin. It is a nature that resists God and His words. It is a nature that behaves independently of God. It is the nature you and I inherited.

Ever since Adam resisted God by disobeying Him in the garden, every descendant of Adam bears that same rebellious and independent nature. In this chapter, I refer to that nature as the "flesh." The NIV Bible calls it the sinful nature. The Amplified Bible refers to it as the carnal, unspiritual nature and as the "human nature without God" (Romans 7:14; Galatians 5:16). Finally the Phillips New Testament in Modern English calls it our "lower nature" (Galatians 5:16). A carnal, fleshly nature is not a kind inheritance.

Nevertheless, you and I came into the world bearing a natural propensity to dismiss God and go our own way. I call it "doing what comes naturally." That is the flesh. And Romans 7:18 tells us there is nothing good in the flesh. Nothing. It always opposes God.

Therefore, it is not surprising that such seemingly sweet people like us can behave in such unholy ways. Something in us is rebellious and self-centered. This is especially noticeable in marriage because the rebellious, self-centered flesh will always fight against the biblical concepts of helping, headship, submission, and respect. It tells our brain that these concepts are nonsense.

The Solution: The Holy Spirit

Great news! God gives us a way out of living by the natural instincts of the flesh. It is living by the power and presence of the Holy Spirit. When we receive Jesus into our lives, a miracle happens. We are spiritually born again (John 3:3). Yes, we are actually born anew with a new nature and a new inheritance, which includes the precious gift of everlasting life.

Meanwhile, because the presence of the Holy Spirit lives in us, we actually have the power to follow the Lord and do what He says. Obedience is now possible. That doesn't mean it is easy or automatic.

What occurs is an on-going battle between the flesh and the Spirit. Every day choices confront you and me to do things either our way or God's way. Galatians 5:17 says, "For the flesh lusts against the Spirit, and the Spirit against the flesh; and these are contrary to one another so that you do not do the things that you wish." But again, the good news is that whereas we once had no power to follow through on obeying God, now the Holy Spirit comes to give us the love, motivation, and strength to do whatever He says. Meanwhile He never condemns us when we disobey. He has paid the price for our sins—our disobedience—and nothing can ever take away His love for us.

Flesh: What It Looks Like

This is where it becomes interesting to me—to be confronted with a situation and realize I have a choice in the way I respond... either in the flesh (doing whatever I want, think, or feel without regard to what God says) or in the Spirit where I say "no" to my flesh and take steps of faith and do what God says.

Here are a few ways the Bible defines works of the flesh: adultery, fornication, hatred, contentions, jealousies, wrath, selfish ambitions, dissensions, envy, murders, drunkenness, evil desire, covetousness, anger, malice, blasphemy, filthy language, and lies (Galatians 5:19–21; Colossians 3:5–9).

Dissension and Anger

Consider dissension—one of the works of the flesh listed above. How might we confront dissension or conflict in our marriage or other relationships? We can either respond in the flesh and keep that dissension alive, or we can respond in the Spirit and do what God says to do, which is to stop talking. Yes, God tells us in Proverbs 17:14, "The beginning of strife is like releasing water; Therefore stop contention before a quarrel starts" (before the dam breaks loose).

Stop. We put our lips together and stop talking. Really? Yes, when we rely on the Holy Spirit, that becomes possible. When God speaks words that sound simple, it is a good time to be childlike and simply trust Him.

Keep in mind that the flesh loves anger and strife. But as a friend says, anger robs our minds of reason. When we (or our husbands or children) don't get our way, we might throw a little tantrum. Let's take to heart this simple word from God to stop dissension by being quiet.

God gives us another way to use our tongues if we need to combat anger or wrath. It is by responding with soft words. The following is a small example, but the principle can be applied to any situation where strife looms.

Years ago, one of our young children had the habit of approaching me while I was preparing dinner, inquiring what was on the menu that night. Unless it was something cheesy or greasy, he would fuss. And of course, I would argue back, telling him how much we need vegetables.

Then one day I discovered Proverbs 15:1, which gives these very practical words from God: "A soft answer turns away wrath, But a harsh word stirs up anger." So the next time our son approached me, I was ready with my soft answer. I simply said, "Oh, I'm so sorry you don't like what I'm cooking. I sure hope I'll have something you like tomorrow night."

Those words stopped him in his tracks. This exchange happened only a couple more times, after which he stopped asking. You can guess why. It became evident he could not engage me in an argument where I was defending every bite of nutrition in that pan. Combating flesh (anger) with the Spirit (a soft answer) has a totally different effect than meeting flesh (anger) with flesh (more anger). So a good way to respond to anger is to speak with a soft answer. Interestingly, both solutions involve how we use our tongues—either to be silent or speak with soft words.

Pride

Another common manifestation of the flesh is pride. Proverbs 13:10 tells us, "By pride comes nothing but strife..." In other words, pride is at the root of strife. And marriage is a ripe area for this to exist. Why? Because neither you nor I want to admit we might be wrong. Instead we fiercely defend ourselves and our opinions, leaving little or no room to seriously consider what our husbands say. Pride does not say, "I'm sorry." And pride does not forgive.

In fact, the flesh never truly forgives. Forgiveness is from God, and the flesh opposes God. It is the Spirit of God who makes this possible. He gives us the grace to forgive in spite of our feelings, even before forgiveness is in our heart. I have learned from experience that heartfelt forgiveness often comes after we have forgiven as an act of obedience. Lest we forget, forgiveness is a choice. We can choose to entertain our flesh by clinging to unforgiveness or humbly seeking God in prayer and making a peace-giving decision to forgive.

How else might pride confront us with the choice of behavior in our marriages? Since the flesh contradicts everything God says to wives, it deceives us into thinking of ourselves as totally self-sufficient independent women. We might think, "Be a helper? I am no man's servant. He's my head? I don't need a head. Submit to my husband? He's not my superior. And show him respect? He doesn't deserve it."

Just imagine how that mindset would affect the way we treat our husbands. In fact, if Madam Fleshy applied for a job, that same way of thinking would likely show up on her application like this:

- I can do the job without help because I am self-sufficient.
- I am adept at being in control because I have much experience.

- I can be relied upon because I am always right.
- I won't need anyone in authority over me because I always know what is best.
- I have total confidence in myself.
- I always do what is right in my own eyes
- I will do whatever is necessary to get the job done.

Romans 8:7 says the carnal, fleshly mind is enmity against God—that is, it is hostile toward Him. So the mind is a battleground. How we think is crucial. Our minds need to be renewed so we begin to think differently—in ways that agree with God. That is what changes and enables us to see that God's ways are perfect. For instance, after many years of teaching and reading about Adam needing a helper (a helpmate), I now actually think of myself as my husband's helper. Well, most of the time. And that comforts both of us.

Lies and Lemon Cream Pie

In addition to strife and pride, lies qualify as a work of the flesh. Would we dare lie? Of course. If it serves our selfish purpose, we will lie. We will lie big, and we will lie little, whatever is convenient. For instance, I have a friend whose husband loves lemon cream pie. One day while my husband and I were in the car with them, I told my friend that I had a wonderful recipe for lemon cream pie. She very quickly quieted me, puckering her lips and whispering, "Shhh! Don't let Sam (not real name) hear you say that! I've told him I don't make that pie because it requires special, expensive equipment." That is the flesh. Just a little lie keeps her from having to bake that pie.

Let's Eat Out Tonight

One fact the Bible makes clear: there is nothing good in the flesh (Romans 7:18). Actually it might look good on the outside and might even behave with kindness at times. But its core is selfish and corrupt. And it is deceptively shrewd in knowing how to get its way.

For instance, one of my friends who doesn't like to cook has a unique means of getting her way at dinnertime. I'm sure her words to her husband sound legitimate, but lurking underneath lies her hidden motive—to get her way. So when she doesn't want to cook, she simply feigns severe allergy symptoms. She even has learned to talk like she has terrible nasal congestion. It works every time, and off she and her husband go to a restaurant. She is merely doing what comes naturally—walking in the flesh to get what she wants.

The devil doesn't force us to misbehave. Instead he tempts us to follow the old self-serving flesh. He makes us think the flesh is good. But the flesh is rotten. And God says those who are in the flesh cannot please Him (Romans 8:8). Cannot.

Flirting

As mentioned previously, sexual sins are listed in the Bible as works of the flesh. I touch on adultery elsewhere in the book, but now let's consider flirting. What do you think the flesh might whisper to the mind of a married person about flirting? Approval! Fun! Intriguing! But flirting among married people is simply a deceptive and illicit means of making one feel attractive and special. Instead our beauty and security are found in belonging to Christ who loves and accepts us just as we are. We need to let that sink in. You and I are loved beyond our comprehension, just as we are.

In His goodness, God tells us how to combat flesh in the area of sexual immorality. Simply stated, He tells us to flee from it. 1 Corinthians 6:18 says it succinctly, "Flee sexual immorality." Move away from it. Abandon it. Run from it. By the grace of God, we can do that. It is a choice. We make a decision.

I once heard a wise teacher say, "Don't ever look at another man the way you look at your husband." Then he added, "And don't let another man look into your eyes in a way that should be reserved for your husband." A Yiddish proverb states it well: "The eyes are the mirror of the soul."

Walking in Newness of Life

> "... even so we also should walk in newness of life"
> (Romans 6:4b).

Now for the good part. "Walk in the Spirit, and you shall not fulfill the lust of the flesh" (Galatians 5:16). To walk in the Spirit is to follow God by faith, doing whatever He says. It is trusting Him and not ourselves one step at a time. It is a process, like learning to walk all over again. We progressively (perhaps very gradually and even painfully) give up some of our old habits and instead begin new ones. In any given circumstance, we now have the power to say "no" to our rebellious ways. We can marvel at not only what Jesus has done for us, but we can marvel at what He is doing in us through His Spirit.

So how might you and I walk in this "newness of life" that God gives to all who believe in Him? It is a challenge because even though Jesus took the fleshly "old us" to the cross where we were crucified with Christ, we are still predisposed to living in the power of human strength, independent of God. Our flesh continues to rise up, begging us to follow.

Red Walls: Pout, Plot, or Pray?

A memorable situation confronted me years ago when I was faced with walking in "newness of life" rather than following my old fleshly habits. At the time I had my heart set on having our white dining room walls painted red, which would necessitate new lighting. (The previous owner had taken the chandelier, and whereas candlelight was sufficient in a white room, it would be inadequate in a red room).

So my husband agreed to my getting bids on recessed lighting, which I did with enthusiasm.

Then the painful moment came. My husband said it was too expensive. That meant we would continue living with dull white walls and candlelight. You can't imagine my disappointment! In my mind I had already seen those red walls and entertained in their midst.

In previous years I most likely would have pouted (or plotted) to get my red walls. But this time I did the right thing. I didn't fuss, argue, or try to convince my husband it was worth the cost. Instead with painful disappointment, I simply said "Okay." As I relinquished my wonderful plans and let go of my red walls, I gave my request to God. I had just died to myself—to my flesh—to what I wanted. It was painful.

Several months later while I was preparing our dining room for guests, my husband walked into the room and said, "You know, this room really does need better lighting." He then said he would get more bids. Thanks to his initiative and efficiency, we now have recessed lighting for a fraction of the original bid. And our dining room has beautiful red walls.

The flesh works hard to get what it wants. But the Christian life is not a struggle to get what we want. It is union with Christ, whereby with prayer and patience we trust Him to give us what He wants. Oh, how we need to resist the urge to push our husbands. That is walking in the flesh, pure and simple. Even if it produces what we want, it is not a victory. Victory comes when we walk by faith, trusting God. That is walking in the Spirit. After all, why would we need to push our husbands if we are trusting God with the situation?

Is there something like my dining room walls you need to let go of and entrust to the Lord? Like wanting a new house, a redecorating job, or even a pet? Incidentally I have wanted a kitten ever since our elderly cat died some months ago. But in a situation similar to having to wait for new lighting in our dining room, I find my husband is not yet ready for another cat. So in spite of my eagerness to get a kitten, I've had to resist pushing for one. I confess, however, that one night

I did mischievously "meow" in bed … several times. My husband was not amused. And that kind of annoyed me because I thought I was funny.

The good news is that the abiding presence of the Holy Spirit helps us make good choices. But learning to make the right choice is a process. Sometimes we obey the promptings from the Spirit, and other times we follow the flesh, which is adept at luring us to do the wrong thing. Those choices are all part of the process of growing as a new person in Christ who is being conformed to His image.

The Saleslady and the Power of God's Word

I end the topic of flesh and Spirit by sharing one of my favorite memories of how God leads us by His Word and Spirit. This time, it was by bringing His words to my mind at just the right time.

It was a dramatic moment. I was about to spiral downward from a disagreement to an argument with a saleslady. I had purchased some leotards and tights, which I was unsure I really liked. But the saleslady said, "They are so comfortable that I'm sure you'll love them. But if not, you can return them."

When I got home, I put them on and quickly decided they were too shiny for me. So I returned to the store the next day. But upon presenting them as a return, the same lady said, "These are not returnable. Can't you see the sign? All sales final." I was stunned.

We had a few unpleasant verbal exchanges that were getting heated when unexpectedly God's word came vividly to my mind: "Love does not insist on its own way" (1 Corinthians 13:5 RSV). My negative feelings did an immediate about-face.

With a different attitude and a softer tone of voice, I said, "Don't worry about it. I'll just keep the clothes." Surprised by my quick turn-about, she asked in a rather harsh tone, "Well, what made you change your mind so fast?"

I told her God reminded me of the scripture, "Love does not insist on its own way." At that, tears filled her eyes. Within minutes, she asked if I would teach her about the Bible. I did, and it was a fruitful time for one reason: God had initiated it by putting that scripture in my mind at the perfect time.

The Holy Spirit is amazing for one reason—He is God—a very personal God who is with us always. When we are sensitive to His voice, we will hear Him bring the needed scripture to our mind at just the right time. It might be "a soft answer turns away wrath…" or …"stop contention before a quarrel starts." Or it might even be, "It is not good for the man to be alone."

Summary

Christian growth is a process. As new creatures in Christ, we gradually learn to recognize the difference between living by the rebellious flesh or the Spirit of God through faith. Meanwhile, we grow in love, faith, knowledge, grace, and learning to please God (Philippians 1:9; 2 Thessalonians 1:3; Colossians 1:10, 2 Corinthians 8:7; 1 Thessalonians 4:1). How encouraging that is!

If you or I ever wish we had faith but we don't, God provides a way to receive faith. Romans 10:17 says, "…faith comes by hearing, and hearing by the word of God." We can settle in with the Bible and ask the Holy Spirit to help us hear God speaking to us in it. A person is speaking the words that are written.

In the beginning, it might seem like only written words. But as the Spirit of God breathes life into those words, we hear Him speaking personally to our hearts. That's when we know God is behind the call to be our husband's helper, to yield to our husbands as our head, and to show our husbands respect. Hearing Him who is invisible enables us to walk by faith. And that is really good.

Therefore, if anyone is in Christ, he is a new creation; Old things have passed away; behold, all things have become new.
—2 Corinthians 5:17

*I have been crucified with Christ; it is no longer I who
live, but Christ lives in me; and the life which I now
live in the flesh (in my body) I live by faith in the Son
of God, who loved me and gave Himself for me.*
—*Galatians 2:20*

Dear Lord, I have befriended the flesh. I have tried every trick in the book to get my way. Please forgive me and help me recognize the many ways I entertain my self-centered flesh in my thoughts and words. Please nudge me when I am about to lie, deceive, argue, or even just exaggerate in order to get my way. Then please give me the grace and power to say "no" to what the flesh is trying to get me to do or say. I am such a self-pleaser that I need lots of help to change my habits. Meanwhile, I can't thank You enough for never condemning me when I mess up.

Please help me live "in newness of life" day by day as I put my faith in You and not in myself. I want to be sensitive to the Holy Spirit's peaceful presence and guidance. Praise You, dear Lord. Amen.

To Submit or Not to Submit?

… submitting to one another in the fear of God.
—Ephesians 5:21

Wives, submit to your own husbands, as to the Lord. For
the husband is head of the wife, as also Christ is head
of the church; and He is the Savior of the body.
—Ephesians 5:22–23

Knowing that the subject of submission is so touchy, one of my friends suggested I not use the word "submit" in the entire book. We agreed the word "yield" sounds much better. But not that much better. Why not? Primarily because that controlling and proud little rebel in us tells us we know best and don't need to submit or yield to anyone. Second, in regard to marriage, the word "submit" might imply that husbands are somehow superior to their wives; therefore the wives' opinions have little value. And finally a big concern comes because submission is often associated with control or abuse, and we know that is not good. So the word "submit" carries a lot of negative connotations. Fortunately biblical submission is none of the above.

Here is the good news: The Lord never teaches the old rebellious part of us to submit to our husbands. It will not submit. It cannot submit. Instead, He teaches the "new" person who has received

Jesus in his or her life. That is the person who has the potential to progressively understand, accept, and apply the call to godly submission (2 Corinthians 5:17).

Most surely, biblical submission is not a one-sided issue. As Ephesians 5:21 says, there is to be an attitude of submissiveness to one another within the whole church. However, within that context, God gives a specific call for wives to submit to their husbands. In a similar manner, Jesus tells the whole church to love one another. And yet He gives a specific call for husbands to love their wives.

My understanding is that at the root of a wife's submission is an attitude of the heart that wants to do the right thing and please the one he or she loves. Jesus submitted to everything His Father asked of Him, even death, because of their love for one another and for us. In fact, Jesus said He only did those things that pleased His Father (John 8:29). So Jesus is the epitome of godly submission.

Let's define three meanings of "submit" and then consider ways to apply them.

Meaning #1: Submit

In Strong's Concordance, "submit" is defined as "to subordinate, to be put under, to be made subject to, to be under obedience." It does not mean being controlled or forced. Submission to our husbands boils down to coming under their authority as our God-given head. It is our response to God's order for the family, not to a husband's demand. As I've heard it wisely stated, submission is voluntary cooperation with another's leadership.

Recently a young friend's husband accepted a job in an outlying area of town that required long commutes in the car. That meant early departures and late arrivals home. He suggested they find a home closer to his office, which would give them more time together and fewer hours of driving time. This was a blow to his young wife because although she knew the benefits of finding a home closer to his office, the thought of giving up her newlywed nest and neighborhood was painful. And yet because she knew what God had said about headship and submission, she knew what was right for her to do. She agreed to move. I know it was painful. And yet her words to me were, "I just want to be a good wife." What an impressive example of a yielded, submitted heart! In today's culture, that might sound foolish. But in today's culture, there are countless strained marriages and ugly divorces.

Consider the turn this new marriage might have taken if my friend had responded in the flesh rather than in the Spirit. She might have pouted, argued, acted like a martyr, or even given him the silent treatment. Instead, by the grace of God she was willing, albeit with a degree of sorrow, to move. She learned a valuable lesson early in her marriage. The lesson is that obedience often involves a sacrifice; sometimes for the husband, other times for the wife. This is discussed in chapter 14.

When our hearts are submitted to God, He gives us the willingness to submit to our husbands when it is appropriate. It is neither blind nor unconditional submission. We are never to submit to sin or evil. Nor are we called to submit to a tyrant or abuser. Our submission should depict and foster union, not division or oppression.

Meaning #2: Subject

In Vine's Expository Dictionary of New Testament Words, the same Greek word for "submit" is "subject." It refers to military rank, as in being subject to the next higher rank. That military reference brings to mind a question I once heard: "Who is the better soldier: the general or the private?" We cannot answer that question without knowing more because the answer does not depend upon rank. It depends upon knowing which one is doing the job assigned to him. If each one is doing his job competently, one is not a better soldier than the other, is he?

So it is in marriage. Our husbands and we have specific roles to accomplish in order to fulfill God's purpose. He's the head; we are the helpers. Neither role is better than the other. They are simply different.

Although we hope our husbands will fulfill their role as competent, responsible, and loving leaders, they might not. But that does not relieve us of our job as helpers who respect them as our God-given head.

Common sense tells us even in business situations, someone needs the authority to make final decisions. The same applies to marriages. That prerogative belongs to our husbands. However, when marriage relationships are right, there is mutual cooperation. Husbands and wives are one flesh under the authority of Christ, not two people in competition. When we think of submission as voluntary cooperation with another's leadership, we think of two working together as one. I appreciate what a friend says: "I see my husband as CEO of our family, and I am the president."

Meaning #3: Defer

Finally the Random House Dictionary defines "submit" as "to defer to another's judgment, opinion, or decision." That is a good definition to remember when we and our husbands cannot reach agreement on an issue. After opinions and concerns have been expressed, the Holy Spirit gives us the grace to defer to our husbands. As I've heard it stated, the husband has the right to break the tie—to end the stalemate. Even though we share the vital role of decision-making, sometimes the act of deferring to our husbands is a god-send. It can lighten the burdensome responsibility for difficult decisions.

A memorable example of this is a situation brought to my attention by a young woman whose divorced mother had ongoing financial problems and often sought help from her children. I was told the mother lived above her means and quickly spent whatever was given to her. After years of helping her out, the son-in-law decided to stop giving money to his mother-in-law.

Filled with anxiety, the young woman said to me, "I don't know what to do. My husband says he is unwilling to give any more money to my mom, but the members of my family are pressuring me to continue joining them in helping her. What should I do?"

I knew whatever she did would be difficult. But I took her to the scriptures to show her how the word "defer" or "submit" could help her. In other words, to whom do we defer or submit— to our siblings or to our husbands? God lightens that burden for us. We can follow the head God gave us, even if we disagree with his judgment or decision, knowing we have obeyed God and that God Himself stands behind our obedience.

I sensed a visible relief in that young woman when she recognized that by His word, God had shown her what to do: "Wives, submit to your own husbands, as to the Lord." Note: it is to our own husband that we yield, not to anyone else's husband. In other words, what her sister's husband said was not to determine her response to her own husband.

I don't know how this played out, but most surely it involved both anguish and diplomacy. What I do know is the young woman knew the right thing to do, and hopefully she sought God in how to present it to her family. Following God's will is not always easy, but it is always right.

So How Do We Submit to Our Husbands?

In general, how are we to submit, subject, and defer to our husbands? The first fact I consider is Ephesians 5:32, which tells us marriage is a mystery that refers to Christ and the church. Therefore, I find it helpful to ask how the church submits to Christ. As discussed in chapter 6, the church looks to Jesus as their head by listening to Him and following (doing) what He says. The principle isn't really that different in marriage. We listen, we speak, and we follow. That is submission—our response to God-given authority.

For me, the biggest test of acknowledging our husband's headship and submitting to that authority comes when we and our husbands disagree on major issues such as money or job or schools. That is when we are called to respectfully hear them out (listen without interrupting) and then respectfully share (not blare) our position.

Our husbands need to know how strongly we feel about our position and how much we want and need for them to value our opinions.

Nevertheless, by the grace of God it is possible for us to comply with our husbands' judgment after they have heard us out and the discussion is ended. As we comply—or submit—it is with the realization that God holds our husbands (not us) responsible for the decisions and direction of our family. That helps bring a degree of peace. God hears us and honors our obedience. We have submitted "as to the Lord"—out of reverence to Him and His words to us.

Certainly there are times our husbands will defer or yield to us. After all, there should be a mutual submissiveness that comes out of a desire to do what is best for the family as well as to please the one we love. So submission is not merely an act of obedience or deference. It is also an attitude of wanting to do the right thing out of love. Our husbands' deference to us neither negates their position as head nor minimizes their responsibility to lead. Nor does any ineptness on their part negate God's call for us to acknowledge them as our head.

By all means, God's instruction to wives to submit to their husbands is not a green light for our husbands to dictate or make all the decisions while we passively sit back and allow ourselves to be controlled. That is not godly submission. We should be free to make many decisions, if not most, on our own. As a pastor-friend explains, a wise husband sees that his responsible wife has great freedom, particularly in areas where she is gifted. He notes that the good wife of Proverbs 31 is a woman active in affairs that require on-the-spot decision-making. Therefore, husbands need not micromanage or be involved in every decision.

Deferring to Expertise

A friend of mine has particularly good negotiating skills. Recently it was time to buy a new car, so her husband deferred to her expertise and asked her to handle the purchase. She was delighted, used her gift, and the car was satisfactorily purchased. That is a healthy relationship. Her talent was used for mutual good.

We are meant to bring out the best in each other. That includes our gifts and talents. My gifts lie in the area of art; my husband's gifts lie in the area of math. So whereas I am usually content to defer to his decisions on financial matters, he is usually comfortable deferring to me in matters of decorating. As an aside, I suggest that as we "decorate" our homes, we consult our husbands regarding the kind of atmosphere they want. A home is a man's castle too. A yielded heart might have to makes some compromises.

Make Room for the Deer Head

I'm reminded of a friend whose husband has a deer head he dearly loves. It is his trophy from a fondly- remembered hunting trip he took many years before they met. Then they met. And married. When my friend talks about those early years of her marriage, she says of the deer head, "I thought, 'Why would I want that old thing in our house? It doesn't fit in with my decorating scheme!'" So the deer head was hung in the garage for many, many years.

One day my friend asked the Lord to give her a heart that was willing to use the deer head as well as the wisdom to know how to use it. As a result, the deer head was brought into the house, and a whole new room was created around it. The end result was an ecstatic husband. Of the many compliments he gave his wife, one still brings tears to her eyes when she talks about it. Tenderly, he told her, "You don't know how much it means to me to have that deer head in here!" It is his favorite room in the house.

Our Cat in a Vulnerable Spot

Without a doubt, deferring to a husband can put us in a vulnerable spot. We want to obey God, yet we do not want to be that proverbial doormat who gets stepped on.

One sunny day I observed our cat lying asleep on the carpet

basking in a warm, soft spot. He was in a position where his back was flat on the carpet, leaving his stomach totally exposed. I thought, *What a picture of trust!* He was in the most vulnerable of positions where he could be either petted or stepped on. But he trusted us. And we can likewise put ourselves in the vulnerable position of yielding because we are trusting God. Submission is a posture that invites God's hand to lead us through our husbands, not an invitation for our husbands to step on us. Being stepped on is not godly submission.

If we are concerned that our submission is ill-advised or unwise and will lead to our being stepped on, crushed, or harmed, we need not only to seek God for help, but we need to seek a godly counselor or pastor for help.

Let's be logical with the words of Ephesians 5:24, "… just as the church is subject to Christ, so let the wives be to their own husbands in everything." Common sense tells us God does not want us to submit to sin or to the devil and his lies. The Lord came to deliver us from sin, and He tells us to resist the devil who works to steal, kill, and destroy. Godly submission is not an opening for an abusive, destructive relationship. Again, if this is an area of concern, we should refuse to submit and should seek godly counsel.

Perhaps the most encouraging and comforting words to embrace regarding the call to godly submission comes from Colossians 3:23–24, "And whatever you do, do it heartily, as to the Lord and not to men, knowing that from the Lord you will receive the reward of the inheritance; for you serve the Lord Christ." That is what makes this teaching palatable. We are sheep following our Good Shepherd. We might never receive praise from our husbands, but our reward is that by obeying the Lord, we have pleased Him.

What we continually face is the fact that marriage is about our relationship with the Lord. He says we are to submit to our husbands "as to the Lord." We are to submit in the context of our faith in Christ, reverence for Him, and obedience to His word. He tells us to submit, so it is ultimately *He* to whom we are submitting. We are learning to honor *Him*. The Lord is changing us to become more and more like *Him*. We are being conformed to *His* image. We are to bear *His* likeness. And Jesus is a man who was fully submitted to His Father as His head, even knowing it meant dying on the cross in our place.

It is beautiful to consider that Hebrews 5:7 (NIV) tells us the reason Jesus's prayers were heard by His Father was because He was reverently submissive. What a statement! I wonder if our husbands would hear us more often if they sensed such a heart in us.

Summary

I will end with a story of my own. Years ago I found wallpaper I thought would look terrific in our entry hall. When I asked my husband's opinion, he said he didn't particularly like the paper, but if I really wanted it, I could go ahead and get it. Although I was disappointed in his opinion, I ordered the paper, telling him he would grow to love it. Finally the paper went up, and I thought it looked fabulous. Occasionally over a period of weeks, I asked, "Don't you think the wallpaper looks pretty good after all?" I never got an affirmative answer from my gentle but honest husband. Do you know what else? I never fully enjoyed that wallpaper.

And isn't that the way it is with God? He loves us ever so dearly, and He gives us His word that we might know the things that please Him. But along the way, He gives us the freedom to choose our behavior. So we make our choice—to please Him or to please ourselves. It is then that we experience either the joy of pleasing Him or, like me with my wallpaper, the futility of pleasing ourselves.

The wallpaper story is not a case of my failure to yield to my husband's headship. I had the green light to get the paper I wanted. But there is something deeper involved. A heart that is truly yielded longs to please. That, to me, is the underlying issue. I could have found wallpaper that we both liked.

When our husbands give us free reign to do whatever pleases us, let's take time to consider what pleases them. That, I believe, is the condition of a truly submitted heart—one that is motivated by love to please the one he or she loves. Our Lord's submission was more than an act. It was an attitude of His heart that manifested itself by humbly yielding to His Father's will.

It is encouraging to know our hope of walking in the blessedness of obedience rests in the Lord's strength and power, not our own. Our gracious Lord is ready and able to help us do His will: wives, submit … as to the Lord. And yes, we can even relinquish the power that comes from having the last word. That is doing what comes supernaturally. That is being an exceptional wife. That is part of keeping our promise to forever love and cherish our husbands. The ways of the Lord are so good.

All the ways of a man are pure in his own eyes, but the Lord
weighs the spirits – the thoughts and intents of the heart.
—Proverbs 16:2 Amplified

Dear Lord, I need Your grace to accept and obey this command to submit to my husband as my head. Please give me the willingness to yield to him out of love for You and obedience to You and your word. Therefore, please give him the wisdom to make good decisions as you help me to stop clinging to my way as if it were the only way. I am trusting that my obedience will open the door for You to work out Your purposes for our family. Thank You, dear Lord. Amen.

Making Submission Possible

God is able to make all grace abound toward you,
that you, always having all sufficiency in all things,
may have an abundance for every good work.
—2 Corinthians 9:8

What Keeps Us from Submitting: Trusting Ourselves Instead of God

That Eve! She messed up everything! Indeed the origin of our reluctance to submit to our husbands goes back to the garden of Eden and the first wife. Why didn't Eve follow Adam's words not to eat from one particular tree? Because she trusted herself, her own senses, more than the words Adam spoke to her. After listening to the serpent and looking at that luscious fruit, she reasoned it was all right to eat it. But she was all wrong. And we are no different than Eve. She is the mother of all living.

What we face now is the challenge to live in the supernatural world of faith whereby we trust God and His words above every ounce of feeling, above every ounce of human wisdom. When God says, "Wives, submit to your own husbands as to the Lord," can we not trust Him with that? As stated previously, submitting "as to the Lord" means submitting out of reverence for Christ, out of faith in

Him, and in obedience to Him. He dearly loves us and is with us to help us "trust and obey."

What He tells us is that without faith, it is impossible to please Him (Hebrews 11:6a). So one way to overcome our reluctance to let our husbands make the final call in any given situation is to take a step of faith and tell God we will trust Him with it. After all, it is He, not our husbands, who tells us to submit. So it boils down to our response to the Lord's words. Remember, the Holy Spirit is our Helper who stands behind God's call to submit. The former chapter covers the fact that we are not called to blind or unconditional submission. We are called to godly submission. Our loving God would never tell us to do something that is not good.

Fear

Coupled with lack of trust is another barrier to submission: fear. We especially fear losing control. We worry that if our husbands have their way, we won't like the result. We simply feel more secure when we think we are in control. That is deceptive. We are secure when we obey. We are God's beloved little creatures who cannot see one minute into the future. Does the Lord not know what is ahead when He says, "Wives, submit …"?

Perhaps we are afraid our husbands' method of disciplining the children is too strict or lenient. And yet, unless there is harm or threat of harm, we do well to stay under the authority of our husbands. After we have privately expressed to our husbands how and why we would handle discipline differently, our job is to prayerfully support our head. As stated previously, if a house is divided against itself, that house cannot stand.

A friend whose marriage was rocky told me her husband and child often argued, and as the self-proclaimed peacemaker in the family, she had to intervene. She feared her husband was too strict with their son, and it made her angry. In time, a marriage counselor stunned her by informing her that she was the problem. She was told to get out of the way and let the father and son work out their differences. She did, and they did. A woman from the marriage class wrote:

> I hadn't realized that fear was my motivation for usurping my husband's rightful leadership role. The Lord is doing a great work in me by releasing me from that fear and enabling me to trust God through my husband to be my head. God has displayed His great, tender mercy and grace toward me by giving me this attitude adjustment before I did any more damage. He is faithfully restoring the years of the locust and opening my eyes to see the wonderful treasure of a husband He has given me.

We must not allow fear to come between God and us. God can surely work in the midst of our marriages when our husbands behave like Adam and don't listen to God. The issue for us is not how well our husbands lead. That is between God and our husbands. The issue for us is our willingness to trust and obey God.

Pride

Another culprit of our failure to submit is pride. Satan appealed to Eve's pride by telling her she would be like God, knowing good and evil if she ate the forbidden fruit. Eve bought the lie and bit it. What might Satan whisper in our ears today that would inflate our egos enough to disobey God? Might he suggest that our husbands are not as wise or spiritual as we are? Or might he suggest that because we earn as much or more money than our husbands do, we don't need to come under their authority?

A particularly ugly display of pride is religious pride. It can devour a marriage. Granted, many wives have more Bible knowledge than their husbands do. But some flaunt it. Others use it against their husbands by telling them how they should behave. As a result, it is not uncommon to see a husband's potential as a spiritual leader get lost behind a wife with an all-knowing or critical disposition.

I remember a woman telling me she was recently divorced. Then she beamed and said, "Yes, I fell in love with Jesus, and my husband couldn't stand it. So he left." That is just the opposite effect a relationship with the Lord should have on our husbands! "Knowledge puffs up, but love edifies" (1 Corinthians 8:1b). Her idea of love for the Lord apparently didn't translate into love for her husband as it should have.

What fruit do our husbands and children see from our relationship with God or our Bible studies? If it is not the fruit of love that builds them up, something is wrong. The purpose of all instruction is love. If God's love and grace don't flow from us, where is God in our lives?

Unfortunately, whereas love and grace come supernaturally from God, pride comes naturally. We always think we are right. We might even make an idol of our opinions. We forget that our husbands also think they are right. Deception comes through pride, so let's not be deceived into believing we are always right. God alone is always right. Notwithstanding critical times such as life-or-death situations, trying to prove we are right can eat away at a relationship. So in the long run, is being right worth damaging or losing an otherwise healthy relationship?

Can you and I be so proud that we are deceived into not submitting? In fact, could Satan be speaking this to us today? (Barbara Spell's paraphrase):

> Now the serpent was more subtle than any beast of the field that the Lord God had made (Genesis 3:1). And he asked the woman if God really said her husband is her head. The woman replied that yes, God says her husband is her head and that she is to submit to him. But the serpent immediately contradicted God's words, telling her that her

husband is really not her head, and she need not submit to him. He pointed out that her husband doesn't live by the Word of God; he has poor judgment; he has no spiritual discernment at all; and he often fails to show her any love. She must lead **him** so that her family will be godly.

So when the woman reasoned that her husband was ignorant of God's Word, and that he didn't take the spiritual lead in the family, and that she was not getting her needs met, she stepped out from under his covering and went her own way. She also criticized her husband, and he went his own way. Then the eyes of both were opened, and they knew they were no longer one flesh.

The answer to pride is humility. That means humbling ourselves before God and our husbands. When we are wrong or sin against them, we need to acknowledge it. We are imperfect wives who are called to submit to imperfect husbands. That's God's way, so let's be wise and accept it. Sometimes the words "please forgive me" might be more welcome than a lovely new negligee.

Disobedient or Unbelieving Husbands

A potential barrier to yielding to our husbands stands before us if our husbands are not Christians. Yet 1 Peter 3:1–2 and 1 Corinthians 7:13–14 tell wives to submit even to disobedient or unbelieving husbands. That is a hard pill to swallow. But God knows what He is doing. Are the Lord's hands tied by unbelieving husbands? With utmost respect, let us remember that God once communicated through a talking donkey (Numbers 22). Can He not also lead through an unspiritual or disobedient husband?

Furthermore, the 1 Corinthians scripture also says the unbelieving husband is sanctified by the wife, just as the unbelieving wife is sanctified by the husband. Oh, how mysterious are the ways of God! Sanctifying here means being set apart. It is as if God has His hand of blessing on unbelieving spouses in a special way by virtue of their oneness with their believing spouses. Amazing!

Meanwhile, it is not living a lie to treat our husbands as if they are our head, is it? In fact, it would be wrong to treat them any other way. The encouragement from 1 Peter 3:1-6 is that a disobedient husband may be won to the Lord without a word from his wife when he sees her reverent and chaste behavior along with a gentle and quiet spirit. That is quite an encouraging scripture, that a wife's behavior might actually draw her husband to the Lord. Granted, there is no guarantee a husband will be won to the Lord by such behavior. The scripture says "may be won." Our job is to behave the way He prescribes and couple it with prayer.

I could cite several cases where women heeded this scripture and stopped talking to their husbands about the Lord. Instead they relied upon the Holy Spirit to make them gracious and attentive wives. Many husbands responded. One returned home after a long separation, one returned home after an affair, and another remarried his wife after the divorce had become final. Why? Fervent prayer was coupled with godly behavior. Those men returned to a place where the love of Christ had become tangible. Even though these are not guaranteed results, we can still be encouraged by them.

I once heard a sermon in which the pastor said, "Don't tell your husband that Jesus loves him until you are ready to love him." In other words, if we have received Christ in our lives, then Jesus and His love are in us. That is what our husbands should see. But are we manifesting that life, that love, to our husbands?

I have a friend who was so eager for her husband to know Jesus that she set all the selection buttons in his car to Christian radio stations. She also placed sticky notes filled with Bible verses all over the house. She now laughs at her futile efforts. The question is: do our husbands see Jesus and His love in us? Or are they just getting sticky notes?

Wives who are unequally yoked with unbelieving husbands might consider this word of encouragement. In the physical realm, there is a time of unseen activity in a woman's body after life is conceived. No one but God in heaven knows the moment of conception. Yet without our knowing it, while the baby in the womb is being formed in secret, those early invisible days of life are being intricately woven. Then after a period of time, there is a physical manifestation. The child conceived in secret is born openly.

In the spiritual realm, perhaps there is a time of unseen activity in the life of unbelieving husbands that you and I don't realize. Only God in heaven knows what is conceived in His kingdom. He initiates everything in the universe, including salvation. Our job is to love our husbands and to pray for them as we wait expectantly for their spiritual birth. May this encourage us to come under the headship of husbands who might be in that invisible stage that precedes new birth.

Poor Role Model

Another reason we might fail to yield is because we grew up in homes where submission, or yielding, was never demonstrated. Therefore, our only role model was a controlling mother. Out of several touching letters from women in the class, this is a portion of one:

> I love my mother dearly and would never do anything to hurt her or cut her down. But I have been praying ever since I was a little girl that I would be different than her and not treat my husband the way she treats my dad. I have even told my dad to let me know if he ever saw me doing it. Then I got married, and I love my husband dearly, but I started seeing it. Then I realized through the class that we all do it (control) because we are flesh. We can't do it (submit) without God's help.

If we identify with the above situation, we can ask God to give us the grace to break such a pattern of behavior as we learn to give up control. That will give our children the gift of a godly role model. One might suggest it was easy for Jesus to come under the authority of His Father because His Father is perfect. But it is quite another matter to yield to a husband who is indifferent, proud, selfish, angry, irresponsible, or lazy. But God can do that through us.

Again, if our submission would result in abuse or destruction to a relationship, we need to be smart and seek counsel.

Summary

The good news is that we are free to submit to our husbands because Jesus Christ can be trusted. He paid a profound price to obtain our freedom to live by faith in Him. Let's be at peace with our obedience. Learning to trust and obey a faithful God is one of the beauties of godly submission. He removes the obstacles of unbelief, fear, and pride that hinder us.

After more than fifty years of marriage, I am convinced that as a general rule, when a husband and wife cannot agree, it is better for the wife to comply with a decision with which she does not agree than not to comply at all. In truth, a husband might be the tool of choice God uses to refine and mature a wife. It is also possible that a wife's submissive attitude is the key God chooses to unlock a husband's hard or indifferent heart. After all, when we display a yielded attitude to our husbands, it likely translates into a display of respect. And that is exactly what our husbands need from us.

God is so good. He is showing us how to keep our promise to love and cherish our husbands whom we married for better or worse. Yielding to our husbands as our head is a beautiful example of showing that love. Frankly, controlling women aren't very attractive.

> *But the wisdom that is from above is first pure,*
> *then peaceable, gentle, willing to yield …*
> *—James 3:17*

Dear Lord, my flesh fights the idea of submission. I have let the lack of trust along with fear, pride, and even other reasons keep me from being willing to acknowledge that You have given the privilege of headship, leadership, to my husband, and when needed, he is entitled to the last word.

Please help me live by faith in You and Your words. I want to replace my hesitancy and fear about submission with faith that You are walking this path with me and mercifully watching over me and taking care of our family. And please give me the peace that comes from knowing I can trust You with my obedience. In Jesus's name, thank You. Amen.

You Mean Respect Regardless?

Nevertheless let each one of you in particular so love his own wife as himself, and let the wife see that she respects her husband.
—Ephesians 5:33

Marvelous news! "Free" marriage counseling! He who created marriage is called our "Wonderful Counselor" (Isaiah 9:6). Speaking through the apostle Paul, this is God's wise and wonderful counsel to every wife: See that you respect your husband. See to it. It's not a suggestion. It's an imperative: See that you respect your husband. How much more emphatically can He say it?

So do you and I respect our husbands? Had I been asked that question several years ago, my quick response would have been a resounding, "Oh yes, I do!" But my answer would have been based entirely on my feelings and opinion of him—that he is a kind, faithful, honest, and trustworthy man of integrity. But what if I paid little attention to him, was bossy, interrupted his sentences, and spent more money than we agreed upon? Could I still say "yes"? Had Eve been asked if she respected Adam, how do you think she would have responded? "Oh absolutely! Adam is great. In fact, he's just perfect!" And then she ate the fruit he told her they were not to eat.

This is the imperative message: respect is not about feelings. It is about behavior—how we treat our husbands. We are to "show" respect. It's an action word.

So What Is Reverence or Respect?

Reverence relates to fear and awe. Respect relates to value or holding in honor or high esteem. Since marriage is about the relationship between Christ and the church, the question I ask is, "What is the primary way we show reverence or respect for the Lord?" I suggest it is by putting Him first. In fact, one might say the fear or reverence of the Lord is related to the first of the Ten Commandments that tells us we are not to have any other gods before Him. He is to be preeminent in our lives.

How does that translate to marriage? My suggestion is that our primary means of showing respect for our husbands is by putting them before any other person on earth. From my observation, this is one of the most common failures of wives. We simply fail to put our husbands first. Why? Because we are naturally self-centered and prone to live by our fleshly feelings. Our flesh will not give our husbands the attention and sense of importance they need.

When we choose to step out in faith and obey God, we are able to put our imperfect husbands first—not ourselves, our children, or our jobs. Our husbands. It's a choice we make. It's not easy, but the Holy Spirit makes it possible.

I remember being at a friend's house when her husband came home at the end of the afternoon. She greeted him quickly with a casual hello. I watched him walk away, having been barely noticed. He looked so alone. Both we and our husbands do well to cultivate the habit of warmly greeting each other at the end of the day. Otherwise, the most ardent greeting we or our husbands might receive comes from the family dog whose fast-wagging tail is shouting, "Glad you're home!" I used to think I was an enthusiastic greeter, but one day when I arrived home from running errands, I listened to the fervent zeal with which I greeted our cat. Our cat! It made me take a look at how I greet my husband.

Attention Getters

Other than putting ourselves first, who or what might we give more attention to than we give to our husbands? At the top of the list is probably our children. And yet, what our children need to see is the devotion and commitment of their parents toward each other. That gives them a sense of security as well as a good role model to follow. Furthermore, by putting our husbands first, we are creating a bond with them (our husbands) that we will especially appreciate when our children are grown and away from home.

Everything from our jobs to our Bible studies can become more important to us than our husbands. I recall watching a woman in the Bible study suddenly realize she had just left her husband at home where he was preparing to leave for a serious doctor's appointment. She was convicted to leave the class and join him for his appointment, realizing he would likely appreciate her presence. How I applaud that woman! She recognized that she had put her Bible study above her husband. Sometimes we just don't think about our husbands and what they might want or need. They need *us*.

Much can stand in the way of our putting our husbands first. Often it is a parent or friend who competes with time that should be reserved for our husbands. Could it be that when we and our husbands unite at the end of the day, our husbands "lose" us to the computer, the phone, or our friends? One pastor told me a common complaint of husbands is that their wives maintain such close contact with their mothers that the husbands perceive they take second place.

A young husband shared with my husband and me how much he used to anticipate coming home at night, but his anticipation slowly waned after repeatedly coming home to a wife who left him to go "out with the girls." He eventually realized his wife preferred her friends over him. It hit him hard. Intimate relationships don't just happen; they involve spending time together.

Consider these thoughts: You and I might have a good grasp of Bible knowledge. We might be gourmet cooks or accomplished athletes. We might be lovely hostesses or great moms. We might homeschool our kids or have responsible jobs. We might keep our bodies in such good shape that we look enviable in our clothes. But is showing respect and paying attention to our husbands a part of these wonderful accomplishments?

The Face of Respect

So what does respect for our husbands look like? It helps to think about what reverence and respect for Jesus looks like. Respect for our husbands is listening attentively. It is valuing their words, opinions, and desires. It is honoring their role as head and letting them lead. It is treating them with kindness. It is speaking positive words that edify, encourage, thank, and praise them. Respect does nothing that would embarrass or harm them.

Respect does not wait for feelings in order to express itself. It sees beyond the surface, knowing that in God's eyes our husbands have eternal value. God loves our husbands. And whereas He wants our husbands to show deep love for us, He wants us to show deep respect for them—regardless. The fact is, we might never realize our desire to have loving husbands and fulfilling marriages, but we can still be good, respectful wives.

Feelings

The continuing problem we have with respect is relating it to our feelings. If we feel our husbands don't deserve our respect, our natural instinct is to withhold it. God is teaching us how to show respect, not how to feel it.

We likely had the utmost respect for our husbands when we married. But marriage is the union of two imperfect people who have very selfish natures. So in time, a husband's shortcomings and habits that were once invisible might begin to glow in the dark (as might ours). That is when our natural response becomes, "I used to respect him, but now I don't," or "I used to love my husband, but now I don't." That translates to "My feelings for my husband have changed."

That is when the Holy Spirit can help us decide to take a step of faith and obey Him. That is when we can say, "By God's grace, I will begin to show my husband respect. I will begin to show him kindness. I will begin to listen to him more carefully." That is the beautiful obedience of faith.

I am particularly thankful my husband doesn't allow his feelings to determine his behavior toward me. For instance, punctuality is important to my husband, and when I run late, I know he is justifiably irritated. Yet even while irritated, he consistently shows me the respect of opening the car door for me.

I realize that gesture might be meaningless to any other woman, but my husband knows I appreciate it. In other words, he shows me respect even if and when I annoy him. Will we not endear ourselves more and more to our husbands if we treat them with such respect even if and when they annoy us? That's where the grace of God comes in. He gives us the power to willingly show undeserved favor to our husbands.

Where would we be without God's favor resting on us? I surely don't want only that which I deserve. And neither does your husband or mine. So let's ask for the grace to forgive and be kind. In fact, unless and until we counter our husbands' sins with forgiveness and grace, we will withhold the respect God said they must have. And if God said they must have it, where does that leave our marriages without it?

The Unloved Wife and Disrespected Husband

Two profound instructions are breathed into the Ephesians 5 passage: husbands, love; wives, respect. By not lumping those instructions together to read, "Husbands and wives, love and respect each other," God is revealing a truth that can easily elude us. Husbands and wives are created with distinct primary needs. Wives need to be shown love. Husbands need to be shown respect. Our husbands have as deep of a need for our respect as we have for their love. How many more ways can God say it?

Lest we forget, a husband's love for his wife and a wife's respect for her husband are meant to reflect that intimate relationship between Christ who sacrificially loves us and us as His bride who reverences Him as the most important person in all of eternity. However, even though we yearn to be sacrificially loved by our husbands, there is no guarantee we will be. The responsibility for a good marriage falls on both husband and wife. We can only do our part. Nevertheless, knowing and doing what God says to us is beautifully rewarding in itself. We learn to depend upon Him, trust Him, and know His deep love for us. Walking in a close relationship with Jesus is our priceless reward.

Beautiful, unloved wives abound. A pastor once told me that he was repeatedly implored by women in his congregation to teach their husbands how to love them. My heart goes out to those women. How beloved they are in God's eyes! Nevertheless, we do well to keep in mind that a husband's failure to love does not negate a wife's responsibility to show him respect.

The unfortunate reality is that just as an unloved wife might become vulnerable to the temptation of a lover outside of marriage, so might a man who is shown little or no respect by his wife. Nearby might lurk the attention and praise of a woman who will give him the respect he craves but is missing at home. Let's not allow someone else to be our husband's number-one fan. "Therefore what God has joined together let not man separate" (Matthew 19:6).

Notice the words "let not." Insofar as it depends upon you and me, we have a God-given responsibility not to let it happen. I know several women who "let it happen." How? Their failure to show their husbands respect at home resulted in their husbands finding respect from women outside of their marriage.

An old song says, "Love and marriage, love and marriage, go together like a horse and carriage." But my version says, "Love and respect, love and respect, are essentials in marriage that husbands and wives mustn't neglect."

The Unlovely Ones

Are we to show respect—regardless? Are we to listen to, follow, thank, and praise an unlovely husband—one whose sin makes him difficult to respect? Yes, even the unlovely ones are due our show of respect. Is not each of us unlovely in some way? Were it not for God's loving kindness, forgiveness, and grace toward us, our sins would leave us forever dead. And that is where our marriages will be without kindness, forgiveness, and grace. So the dilemma for us is to determine how God would have us respond to a difficult husband with proper respect while refusing to condone or encourage his sinful behavior. I am addressing this to wives whose marriages are tolerable yet unpleasant.

One fact stands out in scripture, "… all have sinned and fall short of the glory of God" (Romans 3:23). All. Although each of the following men is commended in Hebrews 11 for his faith, Noah got drunk; Jacob was a liar and deceiver; Moses, about whom it is said he was a friend of God, killed an Egyptian and hid him in the sand; and King David, who is referred to as a man after God's own heart, committed adultery and arranged to have the adulteress' husband killed in battle.

We cannot read that list without realizing God's perspective is unlike ours. These are men who were loved by God. He saw in them something we might not see. "For the Lord does not see as man sees, for man looks at the outward appearance, but the Lord looks at the heart" (1 Samuel 16:7).

God's perspective is eternal, and He alone knows what each person will become. In this life, all things are subject to change. "God … gives life to the dead and calls those things which do not exist as though they did" (Romans 4:17). He called Abraham the father of a multitude before he had even one child.

So if today our husbands drink too much, if they sow lies and deceit, if they are harsh, or if they are womanizers, we need to understand that everything about them and their behavior is subject to change. I know a woman who prayed twenty years for her son who lived on the street as a drunkard. He is now a new man in Christ and pastor of a church. God's lessons are all around us, but one of the most beautiful is that each of His butterflies was once a worm.

Worthy of Prayer: The Power of Intercession

To count an unlovely husband worthy of prayer is one of the dearest of all expressions of respect. We don't need to know if, how, or when our husbands might change. Our job is to love them and pray for them. To neglect praying for a needy husband might be to deprive him of the only intercessor he has on this earth.

I know women who intercede regularly for their unlovely, unpleasant, or otherwise disappointing husbands. Some of the husbands don't yet know the Lord and His love. These wives choose not to allow anger, pain, or sorrow to keep them from forgiving and praying for new life in Christ for their husbands. It is an exceptional wife who is led by the Spirit of God (doing what comes supernaturally) rather than by the flesh (doing what comes naturally).

From my perspective, nothing is more exciting than witnessing the power of the Holy Spirit moving in response to prayer. When the beloved Spirit reaches down in response to prayer to rescue a physical life in front of your eyes (as He has done for me), it is an unforgettable witness to the unfathomable power of His love that works through faith in Him and His name and the power of faith that works through love! Oh, that you and I would know the immeasurable power of His resurrection. Nothing—absolutely nothing—is impossible with God.

Many years ago, a woman shared with me this remarkable story. She said her husband was a weekend alcoholic. (I had never heard of such a thing.) He held a responsible job from Monday through Friday, but once the weekend came, he drank for three days straight. The children tiptoed around the house in order not to disturb Daddy. Often he passed out.

Part of the wife's dilemma was that earlier in their marriage she drank with him, but drinking had now lost its appeal. When she tried to talk to him about his drinking problem, he hurled accusations of self-righteousness at her. What to do? I suggested that she pray according to Isaiah 24:9, that strong drink would become bitter to his taste. I didn't know the woman, and I knew nothing more about her situation until over a year later when I saw her in a bookstore. She relayed the following:

> One evening upon taking his first swallow, my husband grimaced and asked if I had put something into the bottle because it didn't taste right. I hadn't, and I told him that. So he tried drinking from another bottle. He got the same result and again grimaced. On several occasions he made trips to the liquor store to purchase a new bottle. Every time he got the same result. The liquor was distasteful. Eventually he stopped drinking altogether because he said it simply didn't taste right anymore.

Oh, how wondrous is the miraculous power of God moving in response to prayer!

Not a Magic Formula

God cannot be held to a formula. He deals with us individually and uniquely. Even His healings were performed in manifold ways. And whereas some answers to prayer come immediately, others arrive years later.

If we grow tired of praying for or showing respect for a husband in whom we see no change, we do well to read the parable in Luke 18:1–8. Jesus spoke directly to His disciples, telling them always to pray and not lose heart. He knows we become discouraged. And He is telling us how valuable our prayers are. We do well to take Him seriously in His encouragement to persist in prayer.

All relationships are subject to change, and our display of respect might be the catalyst God uses to eventually bring forth love from our husbands. Persevere in prayer. Show respect, regardless. And trust God always.

The following is an excerpt of a letter I received from a woman who said her marriage had been at rock bottom. May it encourage you if your marriage is not what it should be and can be.

> I didn't know how to respect my husband ... I asked God to show me something to compliment my husband on or to build him up. It seemed so strange to daily say something encouraging and nice. Slowly God showed me more and more things to compliment my husband on.
>
> My husband's and my relationship has completely changed in less than two years. God worked slowly at first, and there seemed not to be much progress. He changed me first by helping me die to myself and learn His principles. I was blaming my husband the whole time when I was really not being obedient to be respectful and submissive. God became the most real He has ever been to me by my learning and living the principles of submission and respect.

I include this letter because it gives hope when we don't see immediate changes in our relationship with our husbands even though we are praying and learning to be respectful. This woman and her friend prayed daily for two years. Never lose hope. Her testimony is one of countless ones where women acknowledged that their own hearts and behavior also needed changing.

We might have to swallow our pride and take the initiative in respectful behavior. We can begin with small steps, showing one gesture of respect today and another tomorrow. Let's be kind and willing to speak a word of encouragement—or thanks—or praise.

Summary

Is it possible our husbands have been shown "little" love or "little" respect in the past? Behavior has a cause. "We love because He first loved us" (1 John 4:19). Could it be some men behave disrespectfully because they have never been shown respect? What a blessing to begin showing respect to such a person.

Consider the oyster. When an irritating piece of grit gets inside an oyster, the oyster releases a substance that reacts against the intrusion. It is precisely that substance responding to grit that eventually forms a pearl. Imagine that! So if our husbands are like grit in our lives, God will give us the needed grace to wrap around them with the hope that in time they, too, might become beautiful pearls. We mustn't allow an irritant to keep us from obeying the Lord. When God says, "let the wife see that she respects her husband," would we dare answer God, "but you don't know my husband"?

In the process of writing this book, one of our children was married. As I pondered the relationship between our son and his new wife and the life they would share, my thoughts turned to how I want our daughter-in-law to treat our beloved son. Then the piercing question came to me: Do I want her to treat him the way I treat my husband? I will not forget that question. Most assuredly, I want her to treat him with tender love and respect, adoring and yielding to him as the most wonderful man in the whole world. But then I thought, is that the way I treat my husband? Oh, I hope so! At least most of the time!

What about you? Do you want your son to marry a woman who will treat him the way you treat your husband? Do you want your daughter to treat her husband the way you treat your husband? Perhaps we need to change more than we think. As a parent, I now begin to understand the Father's heart concerning how we as the bride He has chosen for His Son are being trained to love and revere His Son Jesus, our eternal Bridegroom. The two relationships are so gloriously interwoven.

Let's consider the gravity of God's instruction to us. Even though it is natural to withhold respect for our husbands when we think it is undeserved, God equips us to live in the supernatural world of faith whereby we do what He says by faith through His grace and power. That is how we keep our promise to forever love and cherish our husbands. It has nothing to do with our feelings. It is all about how we treat them.

Now to Him who is able to do exceedingly abundantly
above all that we ask or think, according to the power
that works in us, to Him be glory in the church by Christ
Jesus to all generations, forever and ever. Amen.
—Ephesians 3:20–21

Dear Lord, thank You for my husband. I acknowledge with sorrow that I often fail to show him respect. If my efforts to be in control have contributed to his becoming a man I don't respect, please change my heart and mind so I relinquish that control. Please open my eyes to see areas where I am disrespectful. And then prompt me by Your Spirit each day to be attentive and to seize opportunities to affirm him with thanks and praise.

I continue to look to You to intervene in our lives so my husband loves me the way You desire and I show him the respect he needs— regardless of my feelings. Even if I don't get a positive response from my husband when I show him respect, I thank You that I can experience the joy of knowing I have pleased You. Amen.

Respect: The Men Speak

... whatever you want men to do to you, do also to them ...
—Matthew 7:12

Sitting across the table from me at dinner one night was a man whose teachings on marriage are highly regarded. I asked, "If you had one message to give to wives, what would it be?" Without hesitation, he replied, "Learn how to show respect for your husband." After years of teaching and counseling women, that man knew something scores of women don't know—that according to God, a man must have his wife's respect.

The gentleman's response led me to wonder how a man defines respect. Exactly what does respect look like through a husband's eyes? How does he want to be shown respect? To find the answer, I asked fifteen men of various ages the question, "How does a wife best show respect for her husband?" Several of their illuminating answers are written throughout this chapter in bold type. Perhaps without surprise, a wife's respect for her husband looks much the same to a man as our reverence for the Lord looks to God. How dramatic indeed are the parallels between the two relationships!

Answers fell into four categories: leadership, attentiveness, speech, and trust.

Leadership

God says: "My sheep hear My voice ... and they follow Me" (John 10:27). The men said: "Let us lead!"

As we will see, in spite of the many men who renege on their role as head of their wives, many others aspire to be responsible leaders. So how does a wife best show respect for her husband?

> **"Allowing me to be the head by submitting to my leadership."**

> **"What immediately comes to mind is when my wife stands by me and accepts my decision even when she doesn't feel the same way."**

> **"Spiritual leadership is a hard job. It is important for a wife to facilitate her husband by making him feel good about the decisions he makes. She should assure him that in whatever he decides, she will be behind him 100 percent ... and she should have enough confidence to let him fail."**

> **"Do not push, do not second guess, do not undermine his authority."**

> **"She (my wife) taught me how to lead through her submission. She held back from making the final decisions."**

That last statement is worth pondering: "She held back from making the final decisions." Many women can testify that their failure to yield was the stumbling block to their husbands' growth. Once a wife backs off from her habit of taking control, a husband often steps in and assumes the responsibility of leadership.

> **"A wife shows respect by her willingness to accept the fact that her mate is imperfect and that some of the things he does are not always wise or optimal."**

From a single man:

> **"You know a woman respects you when she lets you lead. It gives you confidence in the relationship. I resent it when a woman doesn't let me lead. To be a good follower is showing respect."**

Let's take these responses to heart. Men know they make mistakes and poor judgment calls. Our responses to those mistakes either encourage or discourage them as leaders.

> **"Even at the office, a man has to make decisions based on incomplete information, and because of that, there is always a fog on the decision in knowing if I am doing the right thing. A man needs confirmation in order to feel good about the decisions he has already made."**

In letting our husbands lead us, we are not only respecting and affirming their God-given role as our head, we are affirming our trust in God's plan for the family. For one husband, that meant:

> **"Valuing his opinion on raising children. Although he is not present as often because of work, he is not just boss of business, but head of the family."**

Several men used the word "defer" in their answers. One man said his wife shows him respect in this way:

> **"... in the little things where she defers to me."**
> **"Respect can be shown by a wife asking for advice and opinions on anything and everything, including such mundane things as his preference in the clothes she wears.**

Do we ask and respect our husbands' opinion on anything—from what activities we engage in to what we wear? What about what we wear to bed at night?

Attentiveness

God says: "Blessed is the man who listens to Me" (Proverbs 8:34). The men said: "Pay attention and listen to us!" How does a wife best show respect to her husband?

> **"I think it is by communicating to him by actions or words that he is the most important person in her life."**

One husband's answer reflected the answer of many:

> **"How do women show respect? They listen to you."**

Is that not also a primary way we show reverence to the Lord, by paying close attention to what He says? The two relationships are so beautifully intertwined. God says, "Be still and know that I am God…" (Psalm 46:10). How much closer would we be drawn to the Lord and our husbands if we were still long enough to listen to them? What about the unspoken words that reside in the hearts of our husbands? Are we still long enough to perceive them? Perhaps they are saying, "I'm lonely," or "I'm worried." Let's not forfeit an intimate relationship with our husbands simply because we aren't quiet long enough to hear their heart's cry. I'm told one reason counselors are so popular is because they listen.

Again, a common answer was simply, **"Be a good listener."**

Listening to our husbands might involve criticism. Certainly, neither you nor I want to be criticized. But except for husbands who are unduly critical, we do well to consider that God might be speaking to us through our husband's criticism. Instead of being defensive (our natural response to criticism,) the Holy Spirit might lead us to say, "Maybe you are right. I'll take what you say to heart." Then we can talk to the Lord about it. Perhaps He will lead us to utter those two beautiful words, "I'm sorry."

Even if we want to grow spiritually, we probably don't want to make many changes. It's more natural to want our husbands to change. I've heard it said that whereas many brides begin their walk down the church aisle thinking of the aisle, altar, and hymn, in time those three words become "I'll alter him." But transforming lives is God's territory. It never comes by human effort. Interestingly, a newly-divorced man's advice for showing respect was simply, **"Don't focus on trying to change him."**

Change begets change, and our being the first to change might be the very avenue that leads to a changed husband.

Speech

God says: "Enter into His gates with thanksgiving, and into His courts with praise" (Psalm 100:4a). The men said: "Speak words that edify, thank, and praise us!"

The power of words is so profound that God spoke the world into existence and now upholds all things by His word of power (Hebrews 1:3). But there is another fact about words to consider. Words are like seeds, and within them is the potential for death or life.

Not only can physical life depend upon what comes out of the mouth in blessing, cursing, prayer, and proclamation, but the very life of a relationship can be at stake. A woman relayed to me tearfully that she told her husband one too many times that she didn't need him. One day he walked out and never came back. Her words came back to haunt her.

Consider the words the church is to speak to the Lord. They should be words of continual thanks and praise. Why would it be any different in marriage when marriage is to reflect the relationship between Christ and the church?

Therefore, it is not surprising that when asked how a wife could best show respect for her husband, almost every man referred to how his wife speaks about him or to him.

> **"Compliment them. We (husbands) make so many mistakes that when we do something right, let us know."**
> **"Look for the best in him and praise him."**

How do we speak of our husbands to others? As one who has observed women and their marriages for many years, I offer this opinion as a word of caution: casually sharing with other women the weaknesses in our own husband or marriage is unwise. Why say that which might make someone think less of our husband? Furthermore, when an unfulfilled friend or acquaintance learns there is a weakness in a man or his marriage, she is a potential predator. We need to be careful with whom we share anything that is not edifying. As new creations in Christ, God pours grace on our lips to do that.

> **"Show gratitude with words and actions."**

God says in Ephesians 4:29, "Let no corrupt word proceed out of your mouth, but what is good for necessary edification, that it may impart grace to the hearers." Notice the contrast: when we speak, we are spreading either poison or grace. Corrupt words tear down and are on their way to death. Gracious words build up and nourish one's soul.

> **"By showing that I am worthy, including praise."**
> **"Compliment in public."**

What comes out of our mouths reveals the condition of our heart (Luke 6:45). So the key is having our hearts submitted to Jesus. Meanwhile, His Spirit in us is ready to convict us if and when we are about to let something disrespectful fly out of our mouths.

Let's be sensitive to the Holy Spirit and obey His promptings. When we know our heart isn't right, it is good to ask God to create in us a clean heart and to put a new and right spirit in us according to Psalm 51:10.

> **"Don't criticize or contradict in public."**
> **"Affirm him. Congratulate him."**

One man opened his heart with these words:

> **"A husband needs affirmation in his sex life. He wants to know that he is pleasing you—that he is a good lover. Let him know. Affirm his masculinity. Respect his masculinity by letting him know what he does that is good. Find one thing to praise him for. Then another, then another. Men are more fragile than women think."**

That last statement is eye-opening. May it awaken in us the need to be sensitive to our husbands' often-disguised tender emotions. Oh, that we would not bruise a fragile husband with our words. A father added that a wife should,

> **"build Daddy up to the children. If Dad is late getting home, rather than criticizing, say something positive about how hard Daddy is working."**
>
> **"Be an encourager, and look for the best in him and praise him."**

Let's decide to step out in faith and show respect toward our imperfect husbands with words that edify, thank, and praise them. As one woman wrote, "In taking this step of faith, it helped remind me that God calls me to be obedient to His word, and He will take care of the rest. I can trust God."

"Showing appreciation for him as a provider and protector."

Do we thank our husbands for their provision? How appreciated each word of gratitude at home must be, especially to the man who works in a thankless job. Do we tell our husbands how much they mean to us, how smart they are, how organized they are, or anything that edifies and affirms them? Remember, we are "good things" created to be a blessing to our husbands (Proverbs 18:22).

Trust

God says: "Trust the Lord with all your heart" (Proverbs 3:5). The men said: "Trust us and be trustworthy."

As mentioned previously, at some point in writing this chapter I realized the answers I was hearing from husbands were the same ones the Lord reveals He is looking for in us as *His* bride—those who will listen attentively to Him, follow Him, and honor Him with words of thanksgiving and praise. And now the one that stands perhaps taller than any—those who will trust him.

> **"My wife shows me I am worthy the same way I show God that He is worthy, through my respect toward God with my words, my trust, and my obedience."**
>
> **"In my opinion a wife can best show respect for her husband by the following: trust. This would include trusting his decision-making and his loyalty—his loyalty to her and her loyalty to him."**

Although every wife wants a trustworthy husband, not every husband has proven himself to be one. So how are we to trust our husbands? Where is our ultimate trust to be, in man or in God? Our confidence and security must be in God. It is He alone who knows how to deal with the husbands we deem untrustworthy.

Only God can change the human heart. If we tend to be suspicious or jealous, we can ask the Lord to keep our husband's heart and mind for us alone and to then give us the faith needed to trust Him with our husbands. No one wants our marriages to be based on trust and fidelity more than the Lord. Meanwhile, let's ask Him to help us create the kind of atmosphere in our homes that says to our husbands and children, "Welcome!" and "I love you."

I heard a teacher once say that it is a rare man who will rise above the level of trust his wife places in him. Let's convey trust, not suspicion, to our husbands as we allow our faith and hope to rest in God.

...And Trustworthiness

Then consider the flip side of the word "trust." Not only are we to trust, but we show respect by being trustworthy. Marriage has no place for lies, deceit, or hidden agendas. That includes everything from agreed-upon birth control issues to staying within a budget to following through on our words. If we say, "I'll be back in about an hour," our husbands should be able to count on that. And if we see we are way off target time-wise, a phone message to them might be reassuring.

It is worth remembering that the first thing God says in Proverbs 31:11 about a good or virtuous wife is that the heart of her husband safely trusts her. This is more than just trusting her sexual fidelity. An attractive woman told me she hid money from her husband each month until her secret was discovered. She said confessing the truth to him was painful beyond measure.

The passage continues by saying, "Her husband has full confidence in her and lacks nothing of value. She brings him good, not harm, all the days of her life." What a relationship! He has a wife he knows he can rely on. He values her, knowing she will never do him harm. What security and peace that affords him.

For you and me, part of being trustworthy is guarding the privacy and sanctity of our marriage. We need not unlock or open its doors for the world to see. Friends and family have no right to know details. If we wonder if it is appropriate to share something personal, we can ask ourselves if it would displease or embarrass our husbands—or be grievous to God. My own yardstick about many situations is, "When in doubt, don't." An exception to sharing is when one is seeking godly counsel.

Proverbs 12:4 states, "An excellent wife is the crown of her husband, but she who causes shame is like rottenness in his bones." Note that the antithesis to an excellent wife is the one who causes shame. I can think of nothing that would dishonor a husband more than being sexually unfaithful to him.

If ever we are tempted to flirt with the sin of adultery, the wisest decision we can make is to flee from it before it stings us. Sin always proves disappointing. By God's powerful grace, we can choose to say "no" to sin. We can make that decision and begin to show respect for our husbands regardless of our feelings.

If we have been unfaithful or are now being unfaithful, we can acknowledge that sin to the Lord, repent of it (turn away from it), and accept His forgiveness (1 John 1:9). He will give the strength necessary to turn our back on it. Whereas the good Lord convicts us of our sin, He never condemns us. Guilt and shame are not from God. Instead, by His Spirit He offers His love, grace, power, and strength to run from infidelity like we would run from a killer. He wants us to know the peace and joy that come from being rescued from the quicksand of sin. When Jesus died, He paid the price for every one of our sins. As a result, we need to confess our sin, turn away from it, and receive His loving forgiveness. It's done!

I end by quoting a single man who emphatically said about respect, **"Without it (respect), a relationship can't last."** Then with a bit of laughter, he added, **"That's why I'm still single."** Could that also be the reason why many men who were once married are now single?

Summary

Do we respect ourselves? One husband responded to the issue of respect with these words: **"My view is that she must respect herself. That is the only way she can be content in her own role and responsibilities ... and provide a peaceful and contented household."**

Knowing who we are in Christ—accepted, beloved, forgiven children of God whom He has filled with His powerful life—motivates us and equips us to do whatever He says to do. We don't need to look outside of our relationship with the Lord to find our worth. Knowing Him and His love suffices. So as part of keeping our promise to love and cherish our husbands, let's decide to show our husbands the respect God said they must have. Fifteen men have shared how they believe we might do that.

> *Where there is no counsel, the people fall; But in*
> *the multitude of counselors there is safety.*
> *—Proverbs 11:14*

Dear Lord, please make the practical ways spoken by the men in this chapter resonate within my heart. Make me conscious of tangible ways I can show my husband respect even when it seems undeserved and even when I'm shown neither respect nor love in return. Thank You, dear Lord.

Power Walking Past Stumbling Blocks

Cause me to know the way in which I should
walk For I lift up my soul to You.
—Psalm 143:8b

I have a friend who is tall, beautiful, and graceful. Nevertheless, when she power walks in her neighborhood, she tends to trip on raised portions of sidewalk and crash to the ground. Her last fall resulted in an overnight hospital stay to treat a smashed and broken big toe and a badly wounded hand. Her predicament reminds me how easily you and I can stumble in our marriages because of something we just don't see at the time.

Mercifully in His Word, God shows us stumbling blocks that are likely to trip us up and cause us to fall down on our good intentions as wives. Our job is to identify these blocks and to avoid or remove them. The stumbling blocks addressed in this chapter are unforgiveness, dishonoring parents, failure to leave and cleave, control, and a wrong bedroom attitude.

Block #1: Unforgiveness

"… if you have anything against anyone, forgive him, But if you do not forgive, neither will your Father in heaven forgive your trespasses" (Mark 11:25–26). I was stunned. A dynamic speaker at a luncheon I was attending had just given what I thought was a powerfully convicting message on the subject of forgiveness. At the end of the address, not one but two women at my table casually laughed and said they knew they needed to forgive someone, but it was just too hard. Then their conversation moved elsewhere. They had just shrugged off the whole message, intending to go on with life as usual. They had also just turned their backs on one of life's most precious and freeing gifts: forgiveness, a gift so profound that it cost the very life of Jesus.

Here is the message we must understand: If we hold unforgiveness toward anyone, we have distanced ourselves from God and invited an unseen enemy to trip us up in life. Multitudes of women enter marriage or walk through marriage holding onto unforgiveness as if it were a friend. Quite the contrary, it is an invisible thug walking with us to throw us off balance.

Letting Go of Offenses

This is a simple guarantee: our husbands (and others) will make mistakes and sin against us and we against them. Sin will happen. How we respond is critical. Sin is always the culprit in an unhealthy relationship. Repentance and forgiveness are always the solution. So where does unforgiveness leave us? Face-to-face with an enemy.

One definition of forgiveness is this: pardoning the one who offended us and letting go of the resentment and desire to see the offender punished. Our fleshly nature will resist doing that. We need to be willing to ask the Holy Spirit to help us make the decision to forgive, because holding onto unforgiveness is like sipping poison that is slowly absorbed into our entire system. Nothing can hinder a relationship more.

The most memorable encounter I had regarding unforgiveness occurred during a conversation with a young woman I had recently met. She commented, "There is someone I can never forgive."

When I talked to this woman, I spoke to her about the passage above from Mark 11, along with the passage in Matthew 18:32–35 (KJV). According to that passage, failure to forgive places us in the hand of "tormenters." The NIV calls them "torturers." Clearly they are our enemies.

The young woman listened, but she said nothing and left without a smile. I agreed to see her a week later. At that time she arrived with a big smile and a lively bounce in her step. Although she never verbalized it, I believe in my heart she forgave the person she needed to forgive sometime during the week.

What happened the following week was thrilling. She requested prayer for conception, lamenting her inability to conceive during her several years of marriage. Within one month she was pregnant. Although I cannot prove it, I believe by God's grace, the power of forgiveness created within that young woman not only spiritual life, but physical. She was pregnant with new life inside of her. What I eventually learned was that her husband had betrayed her shortly after their marriage and she had vowed never to forgive him.

This story is not meant to imply that any other woman's failure to conceive is tied to unforgiveness. This is just one story, but certainly an inspiring one. However, there are many causes, both natural and spiritual, for the physical problems we face.

Few turn down human prescriptions for intense pain in the body, yet by not forgiving, many turn down God's prescription for the deeper pain of a rejected, hurting heart. I recall a conversation with a surgeon who remarked how sadly limited he was. He said, "I can cut away various types of disease, but I cannot not touch anger, bitterness, resentment, or jealousy."

Not a Feeling—a Decision

Years ago I had to forgive the woman referred to in chapter 7 who was jealous of me and my marriage—the woman who did not wish me to be happy, healthy—or even alive. I knew if I waited until I felt like forgiving her, I never would. Fortunately I had learned that forgiveness is a decision, not a feeling. So I renounced the negative, unkind feelings that were churning within me and knelt by my bed and audibly forgave her.

I remember telling the Lord how difficult it was for me to forgive Sue (not real name) but I wanted to be obedient to Him. And although I didn't feel in the least like forgiving, as an act of my will, I forgave Sue. I then asked the Lord to please put that forgiveness in my heart. God honored my obedience as He promised in 1 Samuel 2:30. The feeling of distress I had at the thought of my so-called friend waned slowly over several months, but eventually it left altogether. Forgiveness moved from my mouth to my heart.

As in the story above, it is not necessarily a husband who needs to be forgiven. Whether it is a parent, child, sibling, in-law, step-parent, rapist, or even the "other woman," the answer is the same. We must forgive all who have offended us, whether they are dead or alive. Again, forgiveness is a decision, not an emotion.

We might want to share this truth with our husbands. They too might be holding unforgiveness in their heart. And their unforgiveness, likewise, will be detrimental to the marriage. I once heard a teacher say it is "enlightened self-interest" to forgive and that we need to walk with that kind of "self-interest."

How well I remember a telephone call from a young woman in the marriage class. With zeal she reported that after considering God's command to forgive, she called her husband at his office and told him she forgave him for everything. I don't know what the "everything" was. What I do know is that after hearing her words, her husband cried and told her everything was his fault. That evening, he greeted her with flowers. Forgiveness restored their relationship.

Granted, not every situation involving forgiveness will be dramatic or joyous. But being obedient is in itself a victory and becomes its own reward. The woman in that situation later told me that before she forgave her husband, the word "tortured" described her "to a T." Presenting the Lord with our tear-soaked prayers of forgiveness is like unlocking the door of our self-made cages.

Block #2: Dishonoring Parents

"Honor your father and mother, which is the first commandment with promise: that it may be well with you and you may live long on the earth" (Ephesians 6:2–3).

Have we ever considered how profound the words above are? Our failure to honor our parents can actually cause things not to go well for us. If our lives or marriages are not going well, perhaps this is the reason. When God gave us this commandment, He knew every form of sin that parents could inflict upon their children, including alcoholism, neglect, rejection and physical abuse. Yet He still commands us to honor them.

Honor signifies respect. It does not signify approval of behavior. It means we neither do nor say that which would dishonor our parents. They are to be treated with dignity, respect, and kindness just as Jesus treated prostitutes, dishonest tax collectors, and other sinners.

Like forgiveness, honoring our parents is a decision—an act of the will. Therefore, it is futile to wait until we feel like honoring them. Instead we are to walk by faith in God's word that says, "Honor." We reflect God's attitude each time we treat them kindly. Perhaps our kindness toward them will be our parents' first glimpse into the grace of God. It also might be the beginning of a changed life.

Can we truly honor a parent we haven't forgiven? I remember a woman saying even though her parents were now dead, the concept of honoring them still turned her stomach because they had abandoned her as a child. It was now years later, and she still had no peace. After she realized she was living with an unseen enemy named "unforgiveness," she forgave her parents and experienced a peace that had eluded her since childhood.

There is a profound relationship between love and forgiveness that is noted in Luke 7:47: "… her sins which are many, are forgiven, for she loved much. But to whom little is forgiven, the same loves little." In other words, the gratitude the woman had for knowing her many sins were forgiven, resulted in a lavish display of love. Do our husbands, mothers, or dads "love little" (show little love)? Could it be they have not known much forgiveness? What kind of impact could our forgiveness make on them?

Because marriage involves two sets of parents who are to be honored, it is prudent to encourage our spouses to obey this command so they don't miss the benefits of honoring their parents. Finally, in cases where a couple was rebellious at the time of marriage (perhaps getting married against their parents' wishes), it would be good to ask for forgiveness.

We can read and study the Bible every day of our lives. But until we obey it, what has been accomplished? It's like reading the label on a bottle of prescription medicine but then failing to take the pills in the bottle. At the end of it all, we are called to obey God's command to honor our parents regardless of our feelings. Anger and hurt feelings come naturally. The power to forgive comes supernaturally. When we step out in faith and do what He says in spite of how we feel, we are walking in the Spirit and not in the flesh. And that is really good.

Block #3: Failure to Leave and Cleave

"Therefore shall a man leave his father and mother, and shall cleave to his wife; and they shall be one flesh" (Genesis 2:24 KJV).

Too often it is tragic but true. A husband unwittingly places a stumbling block at the entrance to his marriage that leaves his wife bruised and in pain. That stumbling block is his attachment to one or both of his parents—usually to his mother. When I address this subject in a class, I often hear women sniffling. Unfortunately the sorrow of having to share a husband with a possessive mother-in-law is not uncommon.

When God speaks the words in the Genesis passage, He is establishing a criterion for oneness in marriage. The order is important. The man must first leave his previous attachment to his parents so he can then cleave (cling; hold fast) to his wife and enjoy intimacy with her.

In fact, until a man leaves his parents and cleaves to his wife, he has forfeited two things: his place as head of his home and the oneness God intends him to have with his wife. How? By allowing his mother or father to make decisions for him, a husband relinquishes to his parents his role as the leader or head of his wife. His attachment to his parents is like having an intruder in the marriage. The result is an absence of intimacy with his wife.

Unfortunately it is not uncommon for a married son to cling to his mother or father as if he were still under their authority. Or it might be that the parent doesn't let go of the son. Some of the cases I have seen or heard of are almost spooky. Usually the culprit is a controlling, perhaps jealous, mother who cannot bear to release her son to his wife. Her interference might include telling him what to do, making decisions for him, or using manipulative ways to maintain her hold on him. One young woman told me she was completely ignored by her mother-in-law. That was the method used by the possessive mother to exert control.

On the other hand, it might be a father who has an invisible hold on his son due to the son's financial dependency on his parents. The son might not even realize his obligation to his parents causes him to defer to them rather than to his wife.

If we find ourselves in one of these predicaments, it would be good to prayerfully and tenderly talk to our husbands about what God's word says about headship and leaving and cleaving, especially Genesis 2:24 and Ephesians 5:25–33. Then we can discuss ways to tell our parents about the need we have as a couple to make our own decisions, even our own mistakes. But remember, our husbands don't want to be put on the defensive any more than we do. Putting them on the defensive will spell defeat.

This is not a battle to be fought with fleshly weapons such as sharp accusatory tongues. Words can divide us far too fast, so we mustn't allow our words to pierce our husbands' hearts. Instead we can ask God to show us how best to discuss the problem with our husbands while continuing to love, honor, and forgive our in-laws. This is a time to show kindness. The Holy Spirit is with us to help us do that.

What about a wife's role in the "leave and cleave" relationship? Do we sometimes cling so closely to our parents that our husbands feel abandoned? Are we possibly making ourselves difficult to "cleave to"? Our tendency to be bossy or critical is not very appealing to a man hoping his wife would be his greatest fan—and friend.

Finally, if we are mothers who have sons, consider that one rarely hears of a father-in-law problem. If we see in ourselves a tendency to be dominating or possessive, we need to ask God for the grace to let go of our sons (and daughters) and selflessly support their marriages. Until we release our married children, we are going against God, and we will not have peace.

A Beautiful Mother-in-Law

The most tender-hearted words I have heard on the subject came from the wife of a pastor during her son's rehearsal dinner. I believe her words convey the attitude God desires for every parent:

> To Sue (not real name), I publicly proclaim the untying of the symbolic apron strings to release this most precious son to you, his wife.

> To Sam (not real name), I grant you freedom to emotionally leave home and cleave to your wife, and I promise never to undermine your unity and to always uphold and contribute to your oneness.

May those words be ours as well as we ask the Lord to give us such a heart. "Ask, and it will be given to you" (Matthew 7:7).

Block #4: Control

Now to the jumbo stumbling block: control! How easy it comes. How natural it is. Something in us craves being in control. Proverbs 14:1 says, "The wise woman builds her house, but the foolish pulls it down with her hands." Much has already been said about a woman's unhealthy desire to control. The fact is, through our natural habit of being bossy, we can actually pull down our own houses.

My husband and I enjoy hiking some of the Rocky Mountain trails that have been laid out for hikers. Occasionally we encounter boulders on the path that require us to change the direction of our walk. Similarly God has laid a trail, or path, of leadership for our husbands to walk on during marriage. What happens when a husband wants to walk on that path but encounters a boulder emblazoned with the words "controlling wife"? In what direction might he go?

That husband is likely to go in one of two directions: either on the path of abdication or the path of anger. When a wife habitually takes the lead away from her husband, the man might simply throw in the towel and let her have her way. It is easier than arguing. So he abdicates, and she has a weak husband.

On the other hand, when a husband knows God has appointed him to be head, instead of cowering to a domineering wife, he might angrily contend for the position that rightly belongs to him. And then she has an angry husband. It is sad but true—a controlling wife often leaves behind a weak or angry husband. She has not only pulled down her house, but also her husband.

A small but practical area where we can begin changing the habit of taking control is in the car. Rather than telling our husbands which lane to drive in or where to park, we can exercise some powerful verbal discipline by simply "biting our tongue." It totally baffles me that my husband remains in the slowest lane of traffic while cars in other lanes go zooming by. But does it really matter? At the end of the day, neither of us will remember which lane of traffic we drove in. But would we remember an exchange of harsh words? Probably!

Manipulation

A deadly means of control is manipulation. Whereas it is legitimate for us to influence our husbands, it is sinful to abuse that privilege and manipulate them. A woman told me she considered herself to be of great help to her husband in the decision-making process, but her husband accused her of manipulating him. Her question was, "How can I know whether I'm helping or manipulating?" I suggested that she ask herself what her motives are. If she is trying to get her way, she is probably being manipulative. If she is seeking God's will in a situation, she is probably being helpful.

Likewise, you and I need to consider our motives when discussing an issue with our husbands. A woman's power of persuasion over a man is usually strong, and women can learn how to get their way with a man. Crying might work for some women, whereas turning on the charm might work for others. After fifty years of marriage, I know my husband. You probably know yours too. So rather than being manipulative, let's continue learning to say "no" to our flesh when it's trying to get its way.

One of the most unholy ways wives might exert control over their husbands is using the husband's desire for sex as a manipulative tool to get their way. They might simply withhold sexual intimacy until they get what they want. Where did I learn this? From a pastor who told me this is not an uncommon situation. He said he couldn't stress strongly enough how devastating this behavior is to a man. The sexual relationship within marriage is sacred ground. We will regret trampling on it.

If we have established the unhealthy habit of trying to control everything, there is hope. God stands ready to change that destructive pattern of behavior in us as He did for the following woman:

> The class has meant so much to me … Most specifically in my life, it has helped me drop the power struggle that has been such a destructive force in our marriage. I come from a family of divorces. My mother and both of my grandparents were divorced. Women were always "head of the households" there, and I learned those patterns very well. Thanks to God, I am learning a different way.

Just as Jesus loved righteousness and hated wickedness, as we mature in Christ, we begin to see the hideousness of sin and we grow to hate it. In this case, we see the ugliness of being a controller.

I appreciate this suggestion from a friend. She believes there are three stages in identifying sin: before the act, during the act, and after the fact. Regarding control, in the beginning we see the sin after the act—after we have just whisked the lead away from our husbands or connived in order to get our way. Later as we grow, we see the sin right in the middle of the act—and then we realize, "Oh no, there I go again." Finally we mature to the point of seeing the temptation to sin (in this instance, take control) before the act. And then, by the power of the Holy Spirit, we resist. That is a real victory.

Block #5: The Wrong Bedroom Attitude

This might not come as music to a wife's ears, but it is a tune that needs to be sung. The fact is, the men who were kind enough to read the first draft of this manuscript made identical suggestions. Specifically they suggested that I say more about a husband's need for sexual intimacy. In their eyes, a woman's ho-hum attitude about sex is one of the biggest stumbling blocks to a healthy marriage. According to their comments, being available to enjoy mutual sexual intimacy is a challenge for lots and lots of wives. In fact, one pastor told me it is likely the strongest challenge wives face.

This is what God says about the sexual relationship: "Let the husband render to his wife the affection due her, and likewise also the wife to her husband. The wife does not have authority over her own body, but the husband does. And likewise, the husband does not have authority over his own body, but the wife does. Do not deprive one another except with consent for a time, that you may give yourselves to fasting and prayer; and come together again so that Satan does not tempt you because of your lack of self-control" (1 Corinthians 7:3–5).

We need to pay attention to the words just quoted, "and come together again so that Satan does not tempt you because of your lack of self-control." How could Satan tempt our husbands? The need for sex is strong enough in some men that when their wives do not meet their needs, many look elsewhere. Even though such behavior is not justified, stimulation through adultery or pornography is not uncommon. Loose women and internet-accessible pornography await all men and can be the demise of those who have become vulnerable by their wife's lack of attention.

Blessed is the man whose tired wife is willing to give up her desire for sleep in order to be there for her husband. I realize a mommy who has dealt with small children all day is tired—maybe exhausted. But marriage is full of sacrifices. Giving up some sleep to give our husbands the gift of ourselves might be one of those sacrifices.

I appreciate what a friend told me. Often at the end of the day when she is exhausted, she takes a moment to pray for energy before heading to bed. She's thankful for a husband who wants her even when she is droopy-lidded. Even amidst weariness, God is able to help us enjoy the gift of sexual intimacy with our husbands. If we fail to have joy in our sexual lives, we can ask God for that gift.

Our Challenge

Despite our good intentions to love and cherish our husbands, obstacles wait to trip us up. God is so merciful to turn on the spotlight to show us what they are. Our challenge is to acknowledge the obstacles and see that they are removed. Tripping on them is far more serious than the smashed and broken big toe of the friend I mentioned at the beginning of this chapter.

Often walking in the dark is scary for me. Perhaps it's my age or inability to see clearly in the dark, but for whatever reason, I don't always feel sure-footed. Do we realize without God's word and His Spirit, we would walk through marriage in the dark? The only thing that keeps us from stumbling like much of the rest of the world is that God leads us on well-lit paths. With the Lord's help, we can safely "power walk" through marriage. He is our light.

Your word is a lamp to my feet and a light to my path.
—Psalm 119:105

Now to Him who is able to keep you from stumbling ... be glory and majesty, dominion and power, both now and forever.
—Jude 24–25

Dear Lord, please give me eyes to see any invisible stumbling blocks that exist in my marriage and help me remove them. Please give me the willingness to forgive the people I don't feel like forgiving. Show me any way in which I am not honoring my parents or my in-laws. Show me if I put my parents before my husband. Give me the grace needed to willingly let go of control. Help me to enjoy the gift of sexual intimacy even when I am tired. When my flesh rises up to resist doing these things, please prompt me by Your Spirit to obey You despite my feelings. Thank You, dear Lord.

It's a Covenant

Therefore know that the Lord your God, He is God, the faithful
God who keeps covenant and mercy for a thousand generations
with those who love Him and keep his commandments.
—Deuteronomy 7:9

... she is your companion and your wife by covenant.
—Malachi 2:14b

It was the most exciting event in my life, and I was crying. Yes, while everyone else in the church was smiling with delight, I was standing at the altar shedding tears as my soon-to-be husband and I recited our marriage vows.

In hindsight, I believe those tears sprung from an awareness of the sanctity and seriousness of the occasion. We were two people vowing in the presence of God to become united forever. And those promises ended with the sober words, "until we are parted by death."

Like us, many couples sense the sanctity of marriage and the awareness that marriage is a step into the unknown. When we say "for better or for worse," we have no idea what joy or sorrow awaits us.

Behind those promises, however, lies the key that gives us hope. We are entering a covenant before almighty God, committing ourselves and our marriages into His faithful and merciful hands. We are acknowledging that our marriage is based upon our relationship with Jesus Christ, the One in whom we will find our life and joy as a married couple. God's presence with us, His power in us, and His promises to us allow us to bear every difficulty we will face. We are never left alone. We are never helpless. We have someone on our side forever.

A Word about a Marriage Covenant

Countless books have been written about the deep and profound subject of biblical covenants. I am sharing only the very limited portion that I understand as it relates to marriage.

"Covenant" is the single word God uses to define marriage (Malachi 2:14b). Simply stated, a covenant is a binding agreement or commitment between two or more people for the purpose of becoming united. It is the profound way God has chosen to enter into an everlasting relationship with His people. Likewise, it is the way He has chosen for a man and woman to enter into an intimately personal relationship with each other. God Himself is the spiritual presence and witness of the marriage covenant in which the man and woman commit themselves wholly to each other.

Intimacy. Commitment. Union. Promises. How beautiful are these words that describe a biblical covenant. But a word is missing. The word is "sacrifice." Biblical covenants include sacrifices. Oh. Yes, that's what Jesus exemplified for us. He sacrificed His life for us, the greatest mark of love known to man (John 3:16).

Likewise in the covenant of marriage, a close relationship between our husbands and us will inevitably include making sacrifices for each other. Not literally dying for each other, but literally "living" for each other. We give ourselves to each other and become living sacrifices.

That is something our flesh hates to hear. Who delights in sacrificing anything for anyone? Not us. Not our flesh. Who wants to "die" —let go of—or say "no" to what our self-centered flesh wants?

Willingly giving up even an hour of our precious time doesn't come naturally. It comes by the mercies of God through the Holy Spirit.

Indeed the blessing of "living happily ever after" includes the price tag of sacrifice. But God is with us to help us. He convicts us of the sacrifices we might need to make, and He gives us the grace to make them. How dear of the Lord to walk alongside us, guiding us and giving us strength to do what is right. Meanwhile, even if and when we neglect or forget Him, He never condemns us. He understands and forgives us—and keeps on loving us.

BEING A LIVING SACRIFICE

The Universal Sacrifice: Independence and Privacy

So what are some of the sacrifices that might face us in our marriages? One sacrifice applies across the board. We and our husbands will give up a degree of that long-held independence and privacy we had known as single people. How easy it was to do what we wanted, when we wanted, and the way we wanted. We probably asserted (and savored) a sizeable degree of control over our lives. Selfishness smiled and reigned. But once married, our focus shifts to another person to whom we are committed for life. And sometimes that person doesn't meet our expectations. Nevertheless, a degree of sacrifice, or "dying to self," is needed in every marriage.

Sacrificing Our Plans and Preferences

Eventually you and I will likely face a request or opportunity to join our husbands for an event or occasion we don't want to attend. It can be anything from a business trip to a football game, a social gathering, or a visit with relatives. I suggest we should seriously consider making the sacrifice and say "yes." Let's be thankful our husbands want us. Is it not prudent to sacrifice our own plans and desires to be with a husband who wants our presence?

I remember well a friend who unselfishly chose to give up her weekends in order to be with her husband. He had fulfilled his lifelong dream of buying a ranch. With childlike excitement he anticipated spending most of their weekends in those wide-open spaces with his cows and tractor ... and with her!

My friend shared little of his enthusiasm. Nevertheless, she knew how much joy the ranch brought to him, and she knew he wanted her to join him there. So my friend committed herself to take frequent weekend trips to the country, food in hand. She once remarked, "Sometimes it seems like I'm always packing or unpacking for the weekend. It gets tiring, but I know it's the right thing to do. And it makes Sam (not real name) so happy!" She allowed the Spirit of God, not the flesh, to lead her. (It helped that she liked to read, knit, and cook.)

An unexpected result came from my friend's sacrifice. After many years of unenthusiastically attending church in the city as a concession to his wife, Sam got involved in the small rural church near their ranch. One Sunday morning he received Christ into his life. According to my friend, had she not joined him on weekends, it is unlikely he would have gone to church by himself. We do well not to underestimate the importance of every choice we face and every decision we make.

I might add that this woman's husband died recently. Her words to me were, "Barbara, I'm so thankful I spent my weekends with him. I miss him so much."

Different Seasons/Different Sacrifices

As we consider a few faces of sacrifice that greet married couples, we will see that they can change with each season of marriage. For instance, the wife of a graduate student sacrifices spending time with her husband and having his help simply because he needs quiet time to study. The wife of a traveling husband who is away from home during the week sacrifices being able to share the responsibilities and activities of the home and children as well as simply spending time with him. And the wife whose husband has retired, as mine has, sacrifices a degree of the privacy and independence she had become accustomed to five days a week. And yes, that often includes lunch. Regardless of the season of life we are in and the sacrifices that go along with the season, it is good to continually thank God for our husbands.

Sacrificing Outside Activities

Years ago I knew a woman who was extremely involved in her church activities. She was a capable organizer and competent leader who volunteered much time at the church. One day she told me how frustrated she was because her marriage and home life were not doing well at all. She said that was why she loved being at the church because that was where she could use her gifts.

We talked about the possibility that our homes should be the primary place to use our gifts (and then secondly, outside the home.) She took that thought to heart and sometime later decided to change her focus from doing so much church work to doing more "homework." She decreased the time she spent at the church and with a degree of reluctance began to increase her time at home. I don't know all the changes she made, but I'm pretty sure they included giving more attention to her husband, refraining from criticism, and reaching out to show him respect.

Deciding to change her habits was quite a sacrifice for my friend. Why? Because her activities and involvement at church had been a source of compliments from her friends. In contrast, her home was a place void of attention or appreciation. Nevertheless, her desire to stay committed to the marriage covenant prevailed. Eventually through prayer and counseling, the marriage was restored, and she was able to serve in both places. "Unless the Lord builds the house, they labor in vain who build it" (Psalm 127:1). Godly laboring at home is never in vain, even though at times it might seem so.

Let's consider if we are spending too much time on an enjoyable activity because it is an escape from dealing with problems at home. We might need to give up an activity for a while in order to get our homes in order. And that's okay.

Sacrificing Financially

Monetary sacrifices! Not easy. A dear newlywed said to me, "I knew when we married that my husband's income was far below the level I was accustomed to. I told him it would not be a problem. But it is. There's so much I'm used to that I can't have." As I looked into her tear-filled eyes, we talked through what is really important in life. At some point God spoke to her heart, and she said, "I would rather have a husband who loves me and whom I love more than anything money can buy." She was learning early in her marriage that love involves sacrifices. At that season of life, her primary sacrifice was financial.

Sacrificing Time and Energy

I especially remember a friend whose husband was ill for many years. Much was required of her physically and emotionally. Her response to the difficult situation was to live by the words of Colossians 3:23: "And whatever you do, do it heartily, as to the Lord and not to men …" She said to me, "In the last months of my husband's life, when the need to serve him increased, I would carry his tray of food upstairs, saying, "Lord Jesus, I am doing this out of love for You."

Her source of keeping a good attitude was exchanging her weakness for the Lord's strength. As she stayed near her husband and served him, she knew she was, in effect, serving her Lord, being His hands and feet on earth. The joy of the Lord deflected the resentment of having her time, energy, plans, and eventually her husband taken from her. She was an exceptional wife who epitomized what it means to be a living sacrifice.

It is helpful to remember that whatever we do, we are to do it heartily, as to the Lord and not to men. Doing all things "as to Him" changes our attitude and behavior, not only in marriage but in all of life. Whether it is yielding to a husband's unwelcome decision, nurturing a difficult child, or honoring a disappointing parent, it makes all the difference when we do everything out of obedience and reverence for the Lord.

I know a few women whose husbands have become incapacitated in one way or another since marriage. No doubt they have sacrificed in ways I cannot imagine. However, once we see that marriage is not about us but is about our relationship with the Lord, we run to Him for the strength and joy to follow through on our covenant commitment, regardless of our circumstances. We are energized by the reality that "it is no longer I who live, but Christ lives in me" (Galatians 2:20).

Sacrificing Our Strong Wills

And finally there is the sacrifice of our wills. That sacrifice was especially difficult for two of my friends whose natural tendency was to insist on their own way. When they married many years ago, they both knew they were extremely and equally strong-willed. He called her "as strong as horseradish!" He said, "Our personalities were so strong that once a friend approached us in a restaurant and asked, 'How in the world can two generals stay married to each other?' I told him that at the outset of our marriage we decided to rely upon God and one specific promise on which to base our marriage."

The promise by which my friend and his wife lived is in Ephesians 3:20: "God ... is able to do exceedingly abundantly above all that we ask or think, according to the power that works in us." Note the last eight words. My friend said, "We knew it would take the presence and power of the Holy Spirit within us to live in harmony. Otherwise, our marriage would be an ongoing tug-of-war to see whose flesh won the battle of wills."

He continued, "So I asked God for the grace and wisdom to love and lead my wife responsibly without locking horns with her. My wife committed herself to rely upon the Holy Spirit to help her come alongside me as her God-given head without bucking my every move." The result was that through the presence, power, and promises of God, their marriage held together and kept them from continually "locking horns." He concluded, "In spite of many bumps and bruises along the way, we have had a wonderful marriage."

No Guarantees

As we commit ourselves to loving our husbands sacrificially, we hope that they will love us in the same manner. But there is no guarantee. Selfishness is characteristic of every human being. So even though God calls husbands to love their wives just as Christ loved the church and gave (sacrificed) Himself for her, not all husbands are willing or capable to love that way. As a result, the greatest sacrifice some wives make is showing love and respect to a husband who fails to show love and respect in return. How lovingly close God holds those dear wives.

Many women won't have the kind of marriage they hoped for. But they can still be excellent wives who demonstrate their commitment to the marriage covenant through their willingness to make sacrifices when needed. For a wife who feels unloved, simply praising God for His goodness is her beautiful offering, her beautiful sacrifice.

As stated previously, for the one who never marries during her life on earth or the one who never knows a fulfilling marriage, that best-of-all relationship can still be hers—the inestimably precious union with the Bridegroom, Jesus Christ.

Covenant Love

Nothing expresses love like the willingness to sacrifice—or lay down one's life—for another. How does our Father God love us? Enough to willingly sacrifice His Son Jesus on our behalf to pay the price of our sin. And how does Jesus, the Father's sinless Son, love us? Enough to suffer and bleed and die on the cross (in our place) as punishment for the sins of the whole world. These expressions of love are beyond our comprehension.

My husband and I have two beloved sons. When I seriously consider the sacrifice God made of His one and only Son, tears fill my eyes. Surely we can scarcely begin to absorb the depth of His love.

What does that have to do with marriage? Everything. "He who did not spare His own Son, but delivered Him up for us all, how shall He not with Him also freely give us all things?" (Romans 8:32). Those are twenty-seven amazing words. Through Christ, our Father God freely provides everything we will ever need. So how can we receive what He has freely given to us?

A Covenant of Promises

Where can we find the "all things" that God has given us? Where can we find His provision for us? It is there… in His promises! The Bible, His Word, is a treasury of promises! Not simply great promises, but according to 2 Peter 1:2–4, they are "exceedingly great and precious promises." These precious promises are part of our inheritance as God's covenant children. And we are told in 2 Corinthians 1:20 that all the promises of God find their Yes and Amen in Christ. In other words, it is through Jesus that we have the privilege of access to all that God has promised. He and His promises are our life, our hope. So our responsibility and privilege is to find the promise we need at any particular time, meet its condition if there is one, and then receive it with glorious thanksgiving.

Barbara Spell

Clinging to a Promise

Years ago an elderly woman told me how profoundly her life was changed because of one particular promise of God. It seems this dear lady's childhood was characterized by rejection and loneliness. She was moved from place to place and said she always had her bags packed in case she was moved again. As a young woman, she married, but after only a few years her young husband died unexpectedly, leaving her with their very young son who was diagnosed with polio. She said she felt overwhelmed, helpless, and alone.

Somehow (I don't know specifically how) this grieving woman was led to the promise of God in Isaiah 41:10: "Fear not, for I am with you; Be not dismayed, for I am your God. I will strengthen you, Yes, I will help you, I will uphold you with My righteous right hand." She embraced that promise like it was given specifically for her. God did for this woman everything He promised in that scripture. She told me she clung to this promise every day and that it was her anchor for the rest of her life. She lived to be ninety-eight years old. God's beautiful promise was a gift she received and cherished to her dying day.

I remember a friend telling me how much one of God's promises meant to her in a time of fear. It seems there was a rapist loose in her neighborhood. Her husband was out of town, which meant nighttime increased her anxiety. With nerves on end, she prayed to the Lord about her fear and how she needed assurance of her safety. She knew Psalm 91, her favorite psalm. So she read it … and let it sink in. As she clung to the words, she found security in them and became calm, confident that God would protect her. He did.

Often when I experience anxiety, I zero in on God's promise of peace in Philippians 4:6–7. I actually read aloud what He says to do—to stop being so anxious but instead start being thankful as I pray my request to Him. Then at some point, His peace comes. It's not just the words of the promise that make the peace come. It is the person, Jesus, who is behind those words.

When you and I face needs in our lives and our marriages, rather than doing what comes naturally (complain or get angry or nervous), we are invited to go to our heavenly Father and His promises and thank Him and wait for His answer. Fortunately for the person who isn't familiar with His promises, various small books in print contain numerous life-giving promises. It is so good to know and to cling to His promises.

Ending with a Thank-You

So how do we respond to the knowledge that our God is a covenant God who has committed Himself and His Word—His promises—fully to us as His beloved children? We bow in thanksgiving and praise.

I will never forget a Christmas thank-you note my husband and I received from our grandson when he was six-years-old. It was only one sentence long and full of misspelled words. That didn't matter. All that mattered was that he said, "Tanke you." I'm sure our little fella wasn't eager to write us. In fact, he probably was coaxed, perhaps even gently "pushed" into writing. But it still didn't matter. He said, "Tanke you."

As I consider how it warmed my heart to read those two words, I also consider what it must mean to our heavenly Father when one of His children takes time to put aside distractions and say, "Tanke You." Psalm 106:1 says, "Oh give thanks to the Lord, for He is good! His mercy endures forever."

This psalm is clear. It simply gives two reasons to thank God: He is good, and His mercy endures forever. I am touched by the word "mercy" because it connotes both kindness and pity. God knows we are weak and dependent upon Him. Thus, out of goodness and mercy, He gives us everything we need in life through His Son, Holy Spirit, and Word. Even when situations are difficult or seem hopeless, we can trust and thank God for sending His unfailing mercy into that situation. As King David said in Psalm 23:6, "Surely goodness and mercy shall follow me all the days of my life; And I will dwell in the house of the Lord forever."

Meanwhile, God continues to love us, teach us, guide us, and draw us to Himself. What goodness! What mercy! He who died for us will never leave us nor forsake us. And that's a promise! (Hebrews 13:5b).

> *Gather My saints together to Me, those who have*
> *made a covenant with Me by sacrifice.*
> *—Psalm 50:5*

> *For God so loved the world that He gave His only begotten Son, that*
> *whoever believes in Him should not perish but have everlasting life.*
> *—John 3:16*

Dear Father, thank You for committing Yourself fully to me through an everlasting covenant. Thank You for all Your wonderful promises. Thank You for leading me to the promises I need. Thank You for showing me Your principles of marriage for wives, namely helping, headship, submission, and respect. Thank You for giving me the Holy Spirit's power to obey. And thank You for forgiving me when I disobey. Thank You for always loving my husband and me. Amen.

Epilogue

Into the Future

Let us be glad and rejoice and give Him glory, for the marriage of the Lamb has come, and His wife has made herself ready. And to her it was granted to be arrayed in fine linen, clean and bright, for the fine linen is the righteous acts of the saints. Then He said to me, 'Write: Blessed are those who are called to the marriage supper of the Lamb!'
—Revelation 19:7–9

It's All About Him … And It's a Love Story

Life is all about knowing Him: Jesus Christ, the Son of God. History is truly His story. In fact, God's entire written message to humanity, the Bible, is a love story that begins and ends with marriage, from the marriage of Adam and Eve to the marriage supper of the Lamb Jesus with His bride.

The importance of marriage in God's sight is likely beyond our comprehension. We live with a measure of that sense of importance here on earth. Children grow up dreaming of getting married and having children. Parents live in anticipation of the day their children get married. When I was a child, my sister and I walked the sidewalks of our neighborhood pushing our doll buggies while playing "Mary and Frances," two mommies with their babies. (Imagine!—Little girls once had doll buggies!)

Where did that desire for marriage and family come from? I believe it emanated from the very heart of God. Surely even now the heart of heaven beats in anticipation of the marriage of the Son of God to His bride, the church. It will be a family wedding unlike anything known on earth.

God is preparing us for that wedding. Consider the bridal shower and the exuberance of the bride-to-be and her friends as she opens each gift given to her in preparation for her marriage. What is that a picture of? I believe it is a reflection of the excitement and rejoicing in heaven when the Lord showers us, His bride, with gifts of the Spirit in preparation for our life with Jesus Christ.

Do our weddings on earth also have a spiritual counterpart? A foretaste of what is to come? What we know about the first wedding is that the Lord God brought the woman, Eve, to Adam. And that pattern remains to this day. Proud fathers bring their daughters down the church aisle to give (present) them to their husband-to-be. The couple getting married is usually surrounded by family and friends who are there to celebrate and witness the marriage. And the celebration continues with a reception and a feast.

How might that beautiful picture of our earthly wedding ceremonies reflect something yet to come? How might it give us a tiny glimpse into the glory of the heavenly marriage that awaits us? Can we not excitedly foresee our heavenly Father God as the eternal Father of the Bride, who gives (presents) the bride (the church) to His Son, the Bridegroom Jesus Christ? What a picture!

And does this heavenly marriage also have witnesses? Oh, we can hardly envision being surrounded by such an immeasurable throng of heavenly witnesses. And is there a wedding reception in heaven? Oh yes. A feast will follow. The marriage supper of the Lamb has come. It will be a feast unlike anything we can imagine. "Blessed are those who are called to the marriage supper of the Lamb!" (Revelation 19:9).

How awesome it is to consider the heavenly, eternal marriage that awaits the bride of Christ! And as stated previously, for the woman who never marries during her life on earth or the one who never knows a fulfilling marriage, that best-of-all relationship can still be hers—the inestimably precious union with the Bridegroom, Jesus Christ.

Meanwhile

Meanwhile, we stumble, and the Lord picks us up. We try to make it on our own, and we learn the meaning of futility. We seek independence, and we learn how dependent we really are. We reach out to be in control, and we learn our sovereign God is in control. We wrestle with fear, and we learn to trust. We disobey, and we learn His ways are perfect. We realize we are undeserving sinners, and we learn the beauty of grace and forgiveness.

When we step out in obedience, we learn God is faithful. When we behold Jesus and the cross, we see love personified by sacrifice. When we receive His life, we understand freedom and joy. That is when we fall at His feet in worship.

We are the Father's children— His pride and joy—learning, growing, and being disciplined for His glory. We are the Son's bride, learning the profound meaning of covenant love and being conformed to His holy image by the power of the Holy Spirit. In the end, we savor one of the greatest truths of all: nothing can separate us from the love of God, which is in Christ Jesus our Lord (Romans 8:38–39).

With these truths before us and with hearts set on pleasing God, we will find countless ways to say "I love you" to our husbands. Truly, love has no rules. It is simply the presence of God living inside of us, reaching out to embrace. That love comes when we say "I do" to the greatest offer in the world—to receive Jesus Christ as our Lord, Savior, and beloved Bridegroom. How we praise and thank God that He is molding us into the most beautiful bride who ever walked down an aisle.

Now may the God of peace who brought up our Lord Jesus from the dead, that great Shepherd of the sheep, through the blood of the everlasting covenant, make you complete in every good work to do His will, working in you what is well pleasing in His sight, through Jesus Christ, to whom be glory forever and ever. Amen.
—Hebrews 13:20–21.

Thank You, dear Lord. Thank You.

Little Pearls

- It is not good for the man to be alone.
- If it comes naturally, think twice before doing it.
- Marriage is a covenant; not a competition calling for a winner.
- Our husbands need us, regardless of how it seems.
- Love and attentiveness draw husbands home; criticism and nagging repel.
- Independence and intimacy tend to be antithetical. Which are we cultivating?
- Beware of attractive poison. Sin is deceitfully appealing.
- When tempted, think consequentially.
- Well, what does your husband say?"
- Our husbands need us to be their helper; not their teacher, mother, critic, or judge.
- Some husbands can be won to the Lord without a word from their wives. (Shhhhhh. They're looking for respect!)
- Love does not insist on its own way (1 Corinthians 13:5 RSV).
- Forgiving, honoring our parents, and showing respect for our husbands are decisions, not feelings. Waiting for feelings is futile.
- We should pay more attention to our own husband than to any other person on earth.
- Marriage is about our relationship with the Lord (Ephesians 5:31–32.)
- Sin is the culprit of an unhealthy relationship. Repentance and forgiveness are the solution.
- Regardless of how it seems, our husbands need us. At their side. On their side.
- Biblical covenants include making sacrifices.

- It is good to do everything "as to the Lord," ... out of obedience and respect for *Him*.
- Our husband's headship is a gift that provides an invisible covering.
- Cling to God's exceedingly great promises.
- Be sensitive—listen—to the Holy Spirit's promptings. He "talks" to us.
- It's okay for our husbands to have the last word. Really.
- Persevere in prayer. There is a time for all things.
- Our relationship with Jesus Christ is the most important aspect of life and marriage.

Houses and riches are an inheritance from fathers,
But a prudent wife is from the Lord.
—Proverbs 19:14

Printed in the United States
By Bookmasters